THE
INSIDE SCOOP

THE
INSIDE SCOOP
Tips from a Family
Child Care Professional

Chamayne N. Green

Redleaf Press®
www.redleafpress.org
800-423-8309

Published by Redleaf Press
10 Yorkton Court
St. Paul, MN 55117
www.redleafpress.org

First edition 2010
Cover design by Jon Letness
Cover photograph by Steven C. Perkins
Interior typeset in Joanna and designed by Sara Kurak
Interior photos by Andrea L. Underwood and Chamayne N. Green (page 77 bottom)
Printed in the United States of America
16 15 14 13 12 11 10 09   1 2 3 4 5 6 7 8

Library of Congress Cataloging-in-Publication Data
Green, Chamayne N.
   The inside scoop: tips from a family child care professional / Chamayne N. Green.—1st ed.
      p. cm.
   ISBN 978-1-60554-004-7 (alk. paper)
   1. Family day care. 2. Home-based businesses. 3. Early childhood education.
   4. Early childhood education—Parent participation. I. Title.

HQ778.5.G74 2009
362.71'2068—dc22

                           2009014421

Printed on FSC certified paper

FSC
Mixed Sources
Product group from well-managed
forests and other controlled sources

Cert no. SW-COC-002283
www.fsc.org
© 1996 Forest Stewardship Council

To my husband, Tim, and my sons, Maxwell and Braelon,
for your love, patience, and support
of my work with young children and families.

The Inside Scoop

Preface

When I began learning about child development many years ago, I was told to visit many programs, observe children's development, and work hard to become an advocate for children and families. I wrote this book as part of my contribution to advocate for quality family child care programs. Family child care is unique compared to other types of early child care programs because it takes wonderful providers who dedicate their time and are willing to share their homes and families. This dedication allows children the benefit of having a home away from home.

As family child care providers, we are substitute moms and dads, providing intimate care to a small group of children. We wear many hats and juggle our time to effectively meet each child's daily needs. The hours are long and the pay may be small, but the reward of family child care is knowing that we are touching the lives of children in a special way. Our contributions to children's early academic and social foundations will be evident as they become productive citizens in our society. I sincerely hope this book will help you create a path of success and also help ignite or revive your passion for nurturing our youngest citizens. This book is a small token that I offer to help you become successful in your family child care business. Family child care is truly a labor of love.

A special note regarding the use of the word *parents*. Throughout this book I use the term *parents* to represent everyone who is a primary caregiver of children, such as a mother, father, legal guardian, and so on. Parental responsibility is huge, and everyone who acts as a parent in the life of a child deserves respect.

Also, I have alternated the use of masculine and feminine pronouns throughout the text to avoid a gender bias.

Acknowledgments

First and foremost, I thank God for vision, inspiration, and guidance. I am blessed to have the support and love of many people.

I have trained and observed many family child care professionals throughout my career. Thank you for allowing me the opportunity to give advice and in turn receive knowledge and experience working with professionals in the field.

I thank the members of the Child Care Providers' Network for your support throughout my years as president.

I also thank my sister, Carla Anderson, and my great friends, Patricia Barthwell and Chandra Dumas, for being my sounding board and personal editors.

Along the way I have met many advisors, mentors, and early childhood educators in the field who have been a network of support for my personal growth and the success of *The Inside Scoop*. Thank you Reverend Dr. James C. Perkins, the Greater Christ Family, Bob Fenton, Betsy Spiker, Susan Allen, Katrina Stewart, LaShawn Davis, Mingcoria Minter, Candice Smith, Diane Calloway, Lisa Butler, Angela Anderson, Cynthia Jackson, Charlotte Harvey, Gwendolyn Wright, Dr. Sandy Alber, and Dr. Claire Rewold.

I thank my editor, Kristen Kunkel, and the Redleaf Press team, who helped shape and clarify my message to family child care providers.

A special thanks is given to Steve and Kerline Perkins for the cover photograph. The photos for *The Inside Scoop* were taken at Rocking Horse Home Child Care and Academic Adventures. Thank you Andrea Underwood, Stacy Nelson, and Amy Bovee.

I opened Our Place Child Care with the goal of providing high quality care to children in my community. I believe that I reached my goal with the help of my two assistants, Darlene Thomas and Sonya Blackmon. Thank you for joining with me to raise the level of quality child care for the families of Our Place. I would also like to thank you for your hard work and commitment to help Our Place Child Care become an accredited child care home by the National Association of Family Child Care.

A special appreciation is given to the families who allowed me to care for their precious children. The time we shared is priceless.

I believe that I was born with the "entrepreneurial bug." A special thanks to my parents, James Anderson and Helen Anderson, for inspiring me with your business spirit and teaching me the values of hard work and dedication toward business ownership.

Finally, I thank my husband, Tim, my two sons, Maxwell and Braelon, and my Godson, Alex Legion, for sharing your home and my love with the families of Our Place. You have truly been a blessing to me.

1

Making Decisions about Your Business

As a family child care provider, you must make important decisions about your business. First consider whether family child care is the right career choice for you. Ask yourself the following questions to help guide your decision:

- Do I have a passion or desire to work with young children?
- How well do I plan and organize my time?
- Do I get along well with other personalities?
- Can I communicate effectively with adults and children?
- Am I a self-starter?
- Can I physically and mentally handle the daily operations of family child care?
- Can I successfully run the business from my home?

Once you have decided to open a family child care business, there are many details you must consider that will affect the success of your endeavor, including setting your hours of operation, determining the number and ages of children you will care for, planning a curriculum, establishing tuition rates and payment plans, and hiring assistants. Here's a more detailed overview of these considerations.

Set Your Hours of Operation

When setting your hours of operation, consider your family commitments. Determine the hours you can be open for business that won't put unnecessary strain on your family. For example, if most of the activities in your home take place after 6:00 PM, then this would be the ideal time to close each day. Or you may decide that operating your child care business in the evening or during early morning hours works best with your family schedule.

Before setting your hours of operation, you'll also want to consider your prospective families' needs. Speak to families in the area about their schedules, then you can set convenient hours based on their needs. For example, if you live near an assembly plant, there might be requests for child care during the afternoon shift that runs from 3:00 PM to 11:00 PM. Could you accommodate those families? You may live near a bakery whose employees' children need child care from 5:00 AM to 1:00 PM. Would this schedule work for you? In the end you may decide to set your schedule and accept children into your child care within the time frame you create based on your needs. Remember, your hours need not be set in stone. Determine your hours and adjust your schedule to accommodate the families in your program.

Determine the Number of Children You Will Care For

When planning your child care business, you must decide how many children you can accept into your program. Your state child care licensing department has a set capacity for the number of children each child care provider can accommodate. I recommend you start with your state's Department of Human Services Web site, and look under "child care licensing" to get the most accurate information, or you can refer to the appropriate section of your child care licensing manual. In addition, there are two national Web sites that list information:

- The National Child Care Information and Technical Assistance Center Web site (http://nccic.org) has a link for the definition of family child care under "Licensing Regulations."

- The Child Care Aware Web site (www.childcareaware.org) has a listing of each state's licensing department. Look under "Parent Information" then "Licensing" to reach your state's profile.

As a family child care provider, you want to strive to offer quality care for every child. Quality care involves allowing enough space for children to move about freely and participate in a variety of activities throughout the day. It is difficult to offer quality care when you have too many children in your home. No matter what your state's limits are, consider your child care space when deciding how many children you will allow into your program.

Determine the Ages of Children You Will Care For

What ages of children are you going to accept into your program? Infants? Toddlers? Preschoolers? School age? Mixed ages? When making this decision, consider the amount of child care space you have and your comfort level. Understanding the developmental ages and stages of children may also help you decide which age groups will be the best fit in your child care. Many providers take care of their own children as well. If you will be caring for your own children during business hours, ask yourself if your children would feel comfortable in a setting with younger or older children.

Space is another consideration when determining the ages of children you will care for. If you plan to care for infants only, ask yourself how many you can reasonably accommodate. Will you have enough space for cribs or portable bedding as well as a separate safe space for play? Do you want to care for school-age children? If so, is your child care space large enough to support their activities?

Your own feelings are perhaps the most important consideration in deciding which ages of children to care for. There are providers who prefer to limit their care to infants and toddlers because they have a passion for caring for very young children. Do you share that passion, or are you most comfortable caring for preschool or school-age children? Do you feel comfortable caring for all age groups? For some providers, a mixed age group is great, but for others it can be a nightmare. Working with children of mixed ages involves a great deal of multitasking to meet the needs of all the children in the group. Be honest with yourself when making decisions about what ages of children you will care for. If you're not sure, I recommend temporarily working or volunteering with young children at a local family services agency, family child care, or child care center prior to opening your own child care program.

Plan a Curriculum

Deciding what the children will do throughout the day can be a daunting task. As you develop your mission and philosophy statements (see chapter 3), look to them to help guide your curriculum planning. A curriculum is a combination of all of the things we do in a day (see chapter 13). It is a blueprint or instructional path to guide our teaching practices and children's learning. There are many curricula on the market today, and many of them use the same early childhood theories to guide their instruction. Some of the more common curriculum approaches are Reggio Emilia, High/Scope, Big as Life, the Creative Curriculum, Montessori, emergent curriculum, and whole child. You want to choose a curriculum that is appropriate for the ages of children in your care. Some curricula focus on teaching a multicultural and antibias curriculum, while others focus on a play-based approach. Many curricula for child care centers can be adjusted for a family child care setting. There are a host of curricula for home-based child care on the Internet.

The following are keys to choosing and implementing the right curriculum:

1. Choose a program that is structured yet flexible enough to allow for teachable moments and spontaneous learning.
2. Look for a curriculum that limits teacher-directed lessons and activities and encourages child-directed activities.
3. Use the curriculum as a resource as you develop your teaching style, and remember to recognize each child's style of learning.

Grants

Grants provide funding for a specific purpose or goal, and they usually don't require repayment. You may be eligible for a grant to help with start-up costs, equipment costs, special projects, or continuing education. Most grants are available for nonprofit child care programs; however, you may find grants for profit-based child care programs as well. Check with your local child care agencies and human service organizations, such as the United Way, to locate grants in your community.

Family child care programs may also be eligible for grants from major retailers, such as Target or Walmart. The U.S. government also has grants available. Finding grants to help fund projects takes time; start by contacting your local child care resource and referral agency to find out about grants in your area. Be sure to read grants and deadlines carefully to determine if the grant will benefit you and your family child care program. You may decide to write the grant yourself, or you can hire a grant writer. If you decide to use the services of a grant writer, be sure to get professional references.

Establish Tuition Rates

Another major decision you'll make in managing a child care business is choosing how much to charge for the quality child care you provide. Your tuition rates may vary depending on state subsidies and grants as well as on the number of hours you provide care, the number of days you accept children, and charges for early morning or late evening hours. Your location may also influence your tuition rates. If you live in a high-income area, you will probably charge more than if you live in a low-income area. You may also offer extracurricular activities, such as dance, language, karate, art, or music lessons, that change the tuition rate. Just remember that you, rather than the families, should determine the tuition.

To help you set tuition rates, create an estimated budget that lists your monthly fixed expenses (see chapter 7). This information can give you an idea of how much income you must earn to reach a break-even point. Also, check your area for the average rates and the types of child care services provided by competitors to determine if your rates should be higher or lower. Be careful about offering low tuition to attract customers. Your competitors may feel that you are manipulating your prices to steal their customers, and families looking for quality care may wonder how you can offer a quality program when your rates are so low.

Schedule Tuition Payments

Once you set your tuition rate, you need to determine how you want families to pay their child care fees. Most family child care providers have payments for child care set up on a monthly, biweekly, or weekly schedule. You can determine which schedule fits your needs as well as the needs of the majority of your families. A weekly or biweekly schedule seems to be the most popular because most payroll systems are set for employees to receive their paychecks on this schedule. Be sure to decide on the payment schedule at the beginning of enrollment and stay consistent. It is a good idea to set one payment schedule for all of your families to follow. There may be families who request a different schedule to help them maintain their budget; it is your decision whether or not to accept an alternate schedule.

You may choose to accept payment by credit card, by automatic deductions from bank accounts, or by cash, check, or money order. Research the charges you will incur for credit card and automatic check deduction transactions to determine if these fees are reasonable. Depending on the number of children you enroll, you may be able to include this fee in the tuition or charge a service fee for families who choose these transactions. Once you decide when and how you will receive payments, you need to set up a payment collection system. This can be as simple as creating a payment drop box or being available to take payments in person when tuition is due.

Receipt of Payments

Be sure to record all of the payments your families make. Preprint receipts on your computer, or buy them at an office supply store or from Redleaf Press—for example, see the Redleaf Press receipt on page 6. Creating a customized receipt for families is most professional. Document each payment you receive and make a copy of all the checks and money orders for your records. This will help you prepare an end-of-year statement to give to each family for their taxes and will also help you when it's time to prepare your own taxes. You may also want to keep a running total for each month, which will help you when totaling your annual tuition income. See chapter 7 for more information about budgeting.

Determine Deposits and Late Fees

Requesting a deposit for new enrollees is a common practice among providers. Here are several reasons to ask for a deposit:

- A deposit can be used to hold a space in a child care program.

- A deposit can be used to cover administrative expenses.

- A deposit can be used as a down payment on the first week's tuition or held as a security deposit until the family leaves your program. A held deposit may be used to offset an outstanding balance from debt not collected.

In a perfect world, every family would turn in payments on time and pick up their children on time. Unfortunately, families are sometimes late turning in tuition or picking up their children. Although you are a family child care provider, your other responsibility is your own family. You have worked very hard to provide a quality care environment for each child, so please don't feel guilty charging an extra fee for late payments or for late pickups. Consider the fee compensation for the inconvenience of caring for children beyond your hours of operation or for adjusting your monthly expenses to accommodate late payments. If parents don't follow your payment schedule or drop-off and pickup rules, you put in extra time and effort to handle the situation, and you should be paid for that time. Should you charge a forty dollar fee for a late tuition payment? Should you charge two dollars per minute for a late pickup? Consider the value of your time when deciding how much to charge for a late payment or late pickup. See the next section for more guidance on this matter.

Plan for Bad Debt

Family child care providers love to care for children each day, but we become uncomfortable asking families for money owed for nonpayment. Working in this business for a while, I have heard many reasons for late payments: "My check was a little short this week." "I didn't get a chance to cash my check." "I had car trouble and needed to use the tuition to make car repairs." I do try to show compassion for my families, but constantly having late payments is simply intolerable. When a family has a large outstanding balance, it weakens your relationship with them and theirs with you.

As a preventative measure toward reducing the likelihood of bad debt, create a payment schedule that requires tuition payments in advance. Making decisions about how to address and collect debt will also help you enforce your policies. The best strategy in reducing the "late payment syndrome" is to charge a late fee the first time there is late payment. If families are aware that you will consistently enforce your policy, you will see a reduction in late payments. Ensure that the late fee will sting their pocketbooks. It is a consequence for not paying on time. Credit card companies charge a high late fee to ensure their customers will make timely payments. You want your customers to make timely payments as well. As the provider, you don't want the stress of wondering if you will receive enough tuition in a given week to pay your fixed expenses. You want to focus most of your time and energy on the children. When addressing a late payment, I simply inform the family that I have to maintain a quality environment for every child and must have the tuition payment to do so.

There are several ways to collect outstanding balances. For example, you might initiate a conversation about late payments:

- "By the way, Ms. Jackson, I haven't received your child care payment."

- "Mr. Smith, I understand that the cost of child care is expensive. Just imagine how challenging it is for me to operate a quality program."

- "I would hate for Yasil to lose her placement because of nonpayment. She is doing really well here."

You may also want to make a phone call or send an e-mail to remind families of delinquent accounts. A written letter is the most formal approach; an example of a missed payment letter follows.

Use whatever type of message you are comfortable with. At some point, however, you will need to determine when terminating care is the only option.

Your goal is to maintain actively paying families. Be alert to any changes in a family's payment history such as excessive late fees, bounced checks, doubling up on payments, and partial payments.

December 20, 2009

Dear Fred Smith:

I am sending you this letter to request the outstanding balance owed for Rebecca's tuition from December 6 through December 12. You informed me that a payment would be made on Thursday, December 10. I have not received a payment nor have I had the opportunity to personally speak with you. Because of the amount of tuition due, Rebecca may lose her placement at Sunny Skies Child Care. While I would miss having Rebecca in my program, I cannot maintain quality care without timely tuition payments. Please inform me of your intention to resolve this matter as soon as possible.

Sincerely,

Chamayne N. Green,
Director

Plan for Terminating Child Care

There will likely be times when a family decides to leave your program. Therefore, you need to have a procedure in place for terminating care. A two-week written notice is normally required before a family can leave a program. This notice is a courtesy to you because you will need to find another family to replace the family who is leaving. If your contract includes a security deposit up front, the family may not be required to give a two-week notice. If the security deposit you requested will not be used to offset any debt owed, then you may apply this deposit as payment for withdrawal within the two-week time frame. For example, if the family informs you that they will no longer use your service, having this in your contract allows you to keep the deposit.

Remember that it is good business practice to respect a family's decision to terminate care. However, finding out why the decision was made can help you determine if you were a factor and if you need to make any changes to your program.

Sometimes you may decide to terminate care. When this happens, you will need to provide notice to the family via a letter, a phone call, or in person. It is important that you inform them why you made the decision to terminate care. Such a decision should not be made without giving the family advance notice. If you are terminating care for nonpayment, the security deposit should be credited toward their outstanding balance. If the family is leaving your program for other reasons, such as a job loss or a move to another program and their payments are timely, you may have an obligation to return the security deposit.

Hire an Assistant

As your child care business grows, you may need to hire an additional person to help care for the children. Check with your state licensing agency to find out what rules and training requirements assistants must meet. Listed below are tips to help you hire an assistant:

- Create a job description.
- Create an employee handbook.
- Ask family, friends, and child care families for a reference.
- Look for an assistant who has a passion for caring for young children.
- Look for an assistant who is energetic and trustworthy.
- Ask potential candidates to complete an employment application.
- Check a candidate's references.
- Check a candidate's training or experience in child development.
- Complete a criminal background check.
- Take a candidate for a tour of your family child care facility and ask him or her to spend an hour or so working with you in your program to determine whether he or she will be a good fit in your business.

Be sure to follow your state and the federal government payroll tax rules. Also, check if your state requires you to purchase workers' compensation insurance. If you need more information on how to hire an employee, please visit your local library for additional resources.

Now you're off to a great start building a strong foundation for your family child care business. You have many tough decisions to make that will affect how you manage your business. The following chapters provide more assistance to help you become a successful family child care provider.

2

Developing and Writing a Business Plan

A business plan is a guide to help you navigate your business. Writing one will help you develop goals and objectives for your child care business. In addition, a business plan can help you secure a loan from a bank. It can also be used as an assessment tool to analyze your goals, which is a great way to keep you focused during the year. You may want to update your business plan each year to modify any financial figures or goals. You should familiarize yourself with your state's licensing requirements before you write your business plan. For more information on legal requirements, see chapter 4.

While business plans vary, in general you'll want to include the following components: a business description, marketing information, financial management information, and plans for operations. Consider the following information when developing your business plan.

The Business Description

This section of your business plan should include the following guidelines:

- Information about your experience and skills in child care. You may include information about yourself, why you decided to open your child care business, and any skills or training you have received related to child care.

- A detailed description of how your child care business will work.

- The type of business structure you plan on using, such as sole proprietorship, partnership, or corporation. See chapter 4 for more information regarding business structures.

- Your strengths in providing family child care compared with your competitors.

Marketing Information

Include the following information in this section of your business plan:

- Your customer base. Describe prospective families, such as young first-time parents and families with more than one child. Make note of the types of professionals in your area, such as executives, assembly workers, and nurses. Also specify the age range of children you plan to care for.

- Your marketing and advertising strategies. Examples include flyers, business cards, door-to-door visits, signs, Web site listings, and posters. Read about these and more marketing strategies in chapter 5.

- Your tuition rate. You may base this rate on your budget, your location, the services you provide, and the age range of the children you care for. See chapter 1 for more information about setting your tuition rate.

Financial Management Information

This section of your business plan should include the following information:

- The source of your start-up capital needed to open your business. These funds can be from your savings account, borrowed from a relative, or from a loan that you have secured.

- An operating budget showing your estimated first year's expenses. Don't forget to include fixed and variable expenses, such as unexpected grocery trips. See chapter 7 for more information about establishing, tracking, and maintaining a budget.

- Projected income statements. Estimate how much you will receive for the next two years, assuming that you have 80 percent of your expected full enrollment. Include income from tuition, state subsidies, and grants. See chapter 7 for more about state subsidies and chapter 1 for information about grants.

- The name of your accountant. Make sure the person has experience with family child care businesses.

Plans for Operations

Include the following information in this section of your business plan:

- Your child care business management practices.

- Your personnel procedures and hiring practices, in case you need to hire an assistant.

- Legal information and documentation. Examples include your insurance documents, mortgage payments, and licensing forms (as you acquire them).

- An inventory of equipment and supplies purchased for your business. This list will grow as you acquire, add, or update items.

Your business plan can become very detailed. Depending on how you will use it, you may need to include additional information, such as demographics, or quantitative data, such as a cash flow statement and balance sheets. Consult Tom Copeland's *Family Child Care Business Planning Guide* for more detailed information. Your local small business development center can help you write a business plan, and you may find the tips at the U.S. Small Business Administration Web site (www.sba.gov) helpful as well. Remember, a business plan is a flexible document that should change as your child care business grows.

3

Writing Mission and Philosophy Statements

Writing mission and philosophy statements can help you focus the goals of your business. These statements explain to the community what your business's purpose is and should work together to exemplify your passion for and dedication to young children. You will want to share your mission and philosophy statements with the community to help explain your business.

Mission Statement

A mission statement is a clear, concise statement of goals that tells the community why your business exists and what you hope to achieve through it. Your mission statement should be brief; typically a few sentences if used along with a philosophy statement. Mission statements can be changed to meet your needs or the changing needs of child care.

Each child care business is unique, and your mission statement will reflect the goals and values of your particular business. When people read your mission statement, it should give them an understanding of the services you offer. Your mission statement may be a family's first step in determining whether your business is the best fit for them. Here are four examples of mission statements:

- My mission is to provide a nurturing environment that stimulates the development of infants and toddlers.

- Sunny Skies Child Care operates to improve the quality of child care available to families in the Brownstown area. We are committed to providing programs that enrich children's development.

- Sunny Skies Child Care's mission is to provide a nurturing and safe environment for children from birth to age five.

- Our mission is to offer alternative child care services to families in the community who have children with autism.

Philosophy Statement

A philosophy statement helps a potential customer understand your values and beliefs, and it should support your mission statement. Philosophy statements are usually more in-depth than mission statements. Writing one can help focus your business goals and objectives and set the vision for your child care business. Following are two examples of philosophy statements:

- My philosophy is that every child should have a solid foundation in the early years of life. I believe in developing the whole child. I understand the special needs of young children and provide an inclusive environment for them. I provide positive interactions that enhance each child's social, cognitive, creative, physical, and language development.

- Sunny Skies Child Care believes that every child in the Brownstown area should have access to quality child care. We believe that children should have a nurturing and safe environment with developmentally appropriate activities. Sunny Skies Child Care also believes that play is important and children should spend a large portion of their day engaged in play and exploratory activities.

Write Your Statements

The following are a few questions to ask yourself as you prepare to write your statements. These questions will help you narrow your focus in order to write a mission statement and a philosophy statement for your business:

- Why do I want to open this business?

- What are my goals and objectives for this business?

- What contributions will I make to this community through my business?

- How will my business impact the community where I am located?

- What are my beliefs regarding early childhood?
- What type of contribution will I make to the child care field?

It may help to research some of the mission and philosophy statements of businesses in your area. Check for similarities between the business's mission and philosophy statements and how they conduct their business.

Your mission and philosophy statements can certainly change as your business grows; however, I caution against changing these statements too often. Frequent changes reduce the statements' value and may cause some confusion among your families. With that in mind, you may need to revise your statements in order to

- support new child care developments or policies;
- extend services in your business, such as offering transportation or after-school care;
- reflect changing community demographics that may include economic challenges; and
- reflect a change in business status, such as from a sole proprietorship to a corporation.

Share Your Statements

Listed below are several ways you can share your mission and philosophy statements with the community:

- Place them on the cover or in the first section of your family handbook.
- Include them in your business plan.
- Include them when writing grants for the business.
- Frame and hang the statements on the wall of your home-based business.
- Introduce the statements during your family interviews.
- Print them on your fliers and on the back of your business cards.
- List them on your Web site.
- Include them in advertising.
- Use them to secure loans from financial resources.

4

Learning Legal Requirements

Apply for Your License

Before you apply for your child care license, check with your local zoning department for regulations or restrictions regarding opening a child care business in a residential area. This is a critical step in the approval process and may affect your ability to operate a family child care business.

The following is a list of common licensing requirements for a home-based child care program. You need to check with your state to find out exactly what steps you must complete to obtain your license.

- Complete and submit a licensing application.

- Obtain medical clearance for caregivers and household members over the age of eighteen.

- Complete a criminal background check for caregivers and household members over the age of eighteen.

- Complete a home inspection for water, electrical, and heating sources.

- Complete a radon and/or lead test.

- Install fire extinguishers, smoke detectors, and carbon monoxide detectors.

- Complete CPR and first aid training.

- Attend child development training, such as health and safety, child care administration, child development and care, and discipline and guidance.

You will need to determine which areas you would like to use as child care spaces. If you decide to use your basement or the lower level of your home, there may be additional inspections and clearances for appropriate exits or egress windows, smoke detectors, radon levels, and child capacity and to ensure that the area is properly ventilated and approved as a safe place for children. Congratulations! After all inspections and requirements have been met, you can legally set up your family child care business.

Choose Your Business Structure

There are four main types of business structures: sole proprietorship, partnership, limited liability company, and corporation. Each of these business structures has advantages and disadvantages for business owners.

Most family child care businesses operate as a sole proprietorship. This business structure involves one person who owns and operates the business. The owner has complete control of the business but faces unlimited liability. Compared with the other business structures, as a sole proprietor you are responsible for more risk, but you receive more tax deductions.

The partnership structure allows two or more individuals to own a business. There are two types of partnerships, general and limited. In general partnerships, the partners assume responsibility for the debts incurred by the company. A limited partnership, on the other hand, has general partners who run the business and limited partners who are mainly investors.

A limited liability company provides some of the protection of a corporation without the doubled taxes. Earnings and losses are filed on the owners' personal tax returns.

The corporation is more expensive and complex than the other business structures; however, there is also more liability protection. To find out more about the four business structures, read Tom Copeland's *Family Child Care Legal and Insurance Guide* and visit the Internal Revenue Service Web site at www.irs.ustreas.gov.

Name Your Business

Your business name can be as simple as Johnson's Family Child Care or may have a little more whimsical character, such as Our Place Child Care. Your business name will be used on all advertisements, flyers, handbooks, signage, and business documents and when you answer the phone—make sure it rolls easily off the tongue! Choosing the right name for your business may take time. Your name should be simple to pronounce and easy to connect to child care. Brainstorm a few ideas and narrow them down to two or three options. Ask your family to vote on the best name for your family child care business. When you decide on a name for your business, you want to ensure that this name is exclusive to your family child care. Register or certify your business's name with your local, county, or state business office. There may be a small fee to have this name protected from use by other businesses. This type of name protection is usually called a "doing business as" or DBA.

Apply for an Employer Identification Number and a Business Bank Account

You can apply for an Employer Identification Number (EIN) from the Internal Revenue Service online at www.irs.gov or by telephone at 800-829-4933. To apply online, go to www.irs.gov/smallbiz and click on Employer ID Numbers (EINs) to complete the form and receive an EIN. Note: As a sole proprietor, you may use your Social Security number as a substitute for an EIN.

After you receive your EIN, you may apply for a business checking account at your local bank. This is also a great way to track your business expenses and maintain a record separate from your personal bank account. You may also want to open a business savings account at this time. There are many competitive offers for small business accounts. Shop around for the best rates, low bank fees, and freebies.

Tax Considerations

There are many tax considerations when you own and operate a business out of your home.

Form 1040 and Schedule C

When you are self-employed, you are required to file a Schedule C with your Form 1040. For more information, visit www.irs.gov/businesses/small/selfemployed or see IRS Publication 334 Tax Guide for Small Business.

Form 8829 Expenses for Business Use of Your Home

Form 8829 Expenses for Business Use of Your Home is a special form that needs to be filed along with the Schedule C if you live in the home where you work. Form 8829 is used to document the expenses associated with the business use of your home. The expenses documented on this form will come from business use, such as child care space, as well as from personal use. See IRS Publication 587 Business Use of Your Home for more information.

Self-Employment Tax

The self-employment tax is a social security and Medicare tax for self-employed workers. It is similar to the social security and Medicare taxes that companies with-hold from wage earners. For more information about self-employment tax, visit www.irs.gov/businesses/small/article/0,,id=98846,00.html or see IRS Publication 334 Tax Guide for Small Business.

Estimated Taxes

If you have a tax liability one year, you must make estimated tax payments for the next year. Form 1040-ES Estimated Tax for Individuals can help you estimate your tax payments. See IRS Publication 505 Tax Withholding and Estimated Tax for more information.

*Tip | It is very helpful to see a tax accountant or advisor for assistance.

Secure Insurance

It's a good idea to contact insurance companies prior to applying for your license to determine the best rate and coverage. There are companies that will allow you to make monthly or annual payments that are great for small business budgets.

Homeowners Insurance

Please contact your homeowners insurance company to determine if a child care business in your home will be covered in the event of a claim. There are many homeowners insurance companies that will void your policy once they know you have a home-based child care business. You may need to add an endorsement or rider to your existing policy in order to have coverage for your business.

Liability Insurance

In addition to your current homeowners policy, consider obtaining liability insur-ance to protect you in the event of a lawsuit following an accident or incident that occurs in your home. There are some liability insurance companies that also protect you while on field trips. If you are transporting children at any time, you may need additional commercial auto insurance. Contact the Better Business Bureau in your area to inquire about liability insurance companies.

Sexual Molestation Insurance

This insurance will help cover expenses in the event of a lawsuit accusing you of sexual abuse. Sometimes this type of insurance may be included in your liability insurance policy.

*Tip | Please read your entire insurance policy thoroughly. You want to be sure that the policy you buy offers the best protection. Insurance companies have a rating system to assess the quality of insurance. Refer to their rating scales and coverage details before making an investment in insurance.

Now that you have completed the legal paperwork, you can begin preparing your home for children and start informing your family members and friends about your new family child care business.

5

Researching and Marketing Your Niche

Families have several choices when looking for child care. There are many types of
child care programs that offer a variety of services. How can you compete? Find
a niche for your business. A niche can be described as something you do that is
special, unique, or different. It is important to determine your niche early on so
you can cultivate your business with a strong reputation of filling that niche in your
community. As you determine your niche, you may find yourself tailoring your
business plan (see chapter 2) and mission and philosophy statements (see chapter
3) to emphasize it. A niche in the child care business can be as simple as offering
evening care or as complex as having a multilingual curriculum. When determining
your niche, ask yourself these questions:

- What do I do best?
- What can I offer that will set my program apart from others?
- How can I maintain my niche for long-term success?

Know Your Competitors

Before you market your services, you need to know about the other child care
choices families have in your area. Your competitors may include

- centers

- licensed or registered homes

- unregulated homes

- relatives

- charter and private schools

- churches

- corporate on-site programs

- franchises

- public schools

- on-site military programs

With all this competition, you need to have a plan of action to be successful. Find out which types of competitors are in your community and learn all you can about them. Visit their facilities and their Web sites. The following is some of the information you'll want to learn about your competitors.

Competitors' Programming

Do the competitors offer play-based child care, the Montessori method, an academic curriculum, before- and after-school care, sick care, or infant care? Research your competitors' programs and determine if you can offer the same or better programming based on your (potential) families' needs. You can cultivate your niche while seizing the opportunity to offer more choices in your program. Make a realistic assessment to determine if you may lose business because of your program offerings. Is there a heavy demand for infant care in your community? If so, can you provide infant care to support those families and increase your long-term business goals? What about before- and after-school care? Can you meet with your local school district to determine if the district is willing to transport children to your home? How about providing transportation services? There are many children whose parents take the subway, bus, or carpool to and from work. Is it possible for you to pick up children and transport them to your home program? Additionally, research the demographics in your community and be willing to make adjustments to the changing cultural communities within your area.

Competitors' Hours of Operation

Are you losing potential families because the demand for care in your area is for evening hours or during the midnight shift and you only offer daytime care? Are you near a large company whose employees need child care before 6 AM? Are you willing to make changes to accommodate these situations? It's a great idea to speak to the human resource managers in your business district to determine if the companies have high absenteeism because of child care needs and if their employees find it difficult to find child care to accommodate their schedules.

Competitors' Experience

There are many child care programs that have been operating for a number of years. Many families come to know these programs because they are a mainstay in the community. Families know them based on name recognition and possibly because they have served families in the community for many generations. Nevertheless, have they invested in their business and kept up with the latest child care resources and educational opportunities to provide care for families? As a new or seasoned business owner, this is your chance to introduce new technology into your child care program, deliver a different program curriculum, and provide resources that older establishments may not have incorporated. Know how to market your program!

Innovative Services

The Old Way	The New Way
Parents call to check on children	Web cameras show children's activities
Caregivers send letters home	Caregivers e-mail memos and newsletters
Heavy paperwork	Software systems that track attendance, tax forms, meals, and so on and make the data available to families
Weekly cash and check collection	Automatic deductions from checking or credit accounts
Attendance sheets	Swipe-card security systems

If a competing program has been very successful with staying on top of the latest technology, you can still benefit by finding out what makes the program unique and how you can learn from their success.

Competitors' Strengths and Weaknesses

Why are some child care programs in your area so successful? Is it because of family services, quality care, or a great location? No matter how successful the programs are, they likely have weaknesses too. What are the weaknesses? Is there overcrowding, violations, or a gloomy appearance? Make a list of your strengths and weaknesses and those of your competitors to determine if you can benefit from their weaknesses while highlighting your strengths.

Competitors' Reputations

Do families recommend the programs they use? It can be difficult to compete with a home or center that is known for its high quality of child care. You must work hard to show families that your business has many of the services and the high quality of care that your competition has. Tell families about your specialized services. You can also build a reputable child care business by asking for referrals from families.

Competitors' Prices

Does price matter? Yes! It is extremely important to show potential families the value of doing business with you, especially if your prices are higher than your competition. Again, research competitors in your area. Try to find child care programs that are similar to yours and compare prices. Where do you fit? Should you change your price because the center down the street has lower rates? It depends on the situation. Your niche should add value to your program that will help remove the need to set your tuition according to the competition. However, there are times when tuition is the only determining factor between a family choosing you and another child care option. Are major companies closing in your area? Has your community experienced an economic downslide? Should you change your price to help these families? There isn't a right or wrong answer to these questions. You will have to determine if you can play price wars with your competition. For more information about setting tuition, see chapters 1 and 7.

When families visit your home and inform you of their plans to also visit other child care options in the area, be ready to explain why your program is the best choice. Please be courteous and don't slander the competition or spread rumors. Maintain a professional attitude and highlight your program's strengths when comparing your program to your competition.

*Tip | When you are at the park or community center, speak to families with young children. Ask what they do for child care and find out what they like and don't like about their child care situation.

Get the Word Out

Now that you know about your competition, let's take a look at ways to tell people about your fantastic business. Take a chance! Get ready to act!

Be Bold

Break out of the shell of a quiet and passive business person. Family child care providers are sometimes seen as modest, gentle people who move around in society without ruffling feathers. There are many caregivers who have wonderful child care programs but lack the people skills and boldness to tell others about their services. It's time to be an assertive business owner. Tell everyone you know about your business. Next, tell everyone you *don't* know about your business. The more you do this, the easier it gets.

As you tell people about your business, you may meet someone who can help you achieve success. I found a mentor who was willing to help me become just as successful as she was at providing high quality care. I began to research what other high quality programs were doing. I went back to school to pursue my Child Development Associate (CDA) credential and then my master's degree. I submitted an application for my child care program to receive national accreditation. I joined different child care organizations to boost my network of peers and attended conferences to find out more on quality child care standards. Not only did I receive great information, I began to put that information to use. I was bold. I took action! My program has been successful and the majority of my families are from referrals. Reaching your goals takes time and a commitment to achieving results. Don't be afraid to enlist the help of others.

Be Creative

Design a logo for your business. If you need artistic help, hire someone to turn your vision into a real product. Put your logo on flyers, business cards, magnets, and other materials, then take these marketing materials and set up a booth at an event where a large number of potential families will be in attendance. Find other ways to showcase your business; for example, join with other businesses in your area to help sponsor a child-related event or invite local politicians and news media into your program for a special reading event.

Be Realistic

Rather than waiting for an opportunity to come knocking at your door, set up small goals to achieve results. You can't wait for an ideal situation to appear. You may not have the perfect situation to reach your full potential, but you can focus on three or four attributes that will help you obtain quick results. As a new business owner, you may not have the prime location to reach the ideal client base, but you do have special programs, great curriculum, and a quality setting. Advertise your strengths. Highlight all of the wonderful activities the children do in a day and emphasize the quality of child care services. Families have been known to drive out of their way to reach a quality program.

After you have achieved success, you can consider moving to a different location to maximize your results. In my first family child care home, I had limited space and the home needed a lot of renovations. After years in the business, I was able to move to a location closer to my client base and near major freeways. My child care space is larger and I have renovated the space to accommodate all of my child care needs. I took my current attributes and grew my business until I could achieve my long-term goals.

More Marketing Strategies

There are many ways to seek new families for your business. What follows are ideas that I and others in the field have found to be successful. Some of these can be expensive while others require only your time. Try out several and see which ones give you the most responses. Keep track of which method yielded the most business. Remember, it takes money to make money. Marketing your business is time and money well spent.

- Showcase your program by sponsoring an event or setting up a booth with a make-and-take art or science activity at a community festival for young children.

- Hand out magnets, flyers, and business cards to everyone you meet.

- Meet with corporations to let them know you are available to the families of their employees. Consider offering an employee discount.

- Family child care providers can purchase a lawn sign or place a sign in the front window. Be sure to follow city ordinances.

- Car magnets are easy to remove and a great way to advertise. Park at the end of your driveway for visibility during peak times.

- Advertise in the welcome packet for all new housing developments in your area.

- Advertise in the marketing mailers sent to the homes in your community. Watch the pricing for this type of ad. To cut the cost, advertise with another child-related business, such a local toy store or a children's clothing store.

- Advertise in the local yellow pages.

- Post signs in your local markets and parent-friendly restaurants. Also post signs at your local community centers, parks, and playgrounds.

- Set up a Web site that highlights your program.

- Volunteer at local schools, and bring the children in your care to school and community functions dressed in their child care T-shirts.

- Participate in the local parent-teacher association (PTA) fundraisers.

- Knock on doors in the neighborhood and business district. Tell them about your business or leave a business card. You never know who may refer someone to your business.

- Be visible in the community. Volunteer for community groups and network with community members.

- Ask your local hospital if you can place a flyer or business card in the baby packets for new parents.

- Send a congratulatory note and a business card to residents with the famous "stork sign" on their lawn welcoming a new baby.

- Post flyers at various businesses in the community. Be sure to ask permission first.

- Offer a referral discount. When an existing family brings in a new family, the first family gets a one-time tuition discount.

- Of course, word of mouth is the best way to get families.

- Remember, it is easier to keep a family than to gain a new one. Continue to cultivate the relationships you have while working on increasing your client base.

For more information on strengthening the caregiver-family relationship, see chapter 10.

*Tip | You must continue to market your child care business even if you have reached full capacity. There are always upward and downward swings in this business.

6

Keeping Records

There are several methods for maintaining records in a family child care business. A great start is to purchase a file cabinet and file folders. Label the contents of each file folder; for example, enrollment information, attendance sheets, children's developmental records, menus, fire drill logs, or other records. Keep reading for tips on how to maintain accurate records.

Collect and Maintain Child Enrollment Information

When you enroll a child into your program, you will need to collect a variety of documents from the child's parents. Properly maintaining and storing these documents is critical. One way to ensure you have all the necessary documents is to mark them off a checklist of items at the time of enrollment. See page 29 for a sample checklist.

Most of these forms are provided by your state licensing department. In Michigan, for example, the licensing department has specific information on its forms and it requires that providers use the state-issued forms.

Child's name: Todd Reynolds
Date: February 1, 2010

☑ child information card
☑ application and registration forms
☑ family handbook agreement
☑ physical exam forms
☑ immunization record or waiver
☑ medication forms
☑ application for the Food Program
☑ child care subsidy authorization and payment forms
☑ documentation of incidents, accidents, and injuries
☑ any additional forms required by the state licensing agency

Attendance Sheets

There are many family child care providers who feel that attendance sheets are unnecessary. I disagree. Here are several reasons I have for keeping accurate attendance sheets:

- Several states require attendance sheets as a legal record for state child care subsidies.

- Attendance sheets serve as a record for child care tuition payments.

- Attendance sheets that include arrival and departure times can be used to resolve conflicts over late pickups.

- Attendance sheets can act as an additional record of attendance for the Food Program.

- Attendance sheets can verify attendance and/or a parent's signature in a child custody proceeding.

- Attendance sheets can verify attendance in a provider-parent court proceeding.

- In the event of an emergency, attendance sheets should be used to confirm a child head count.

- Attendance sheets can double as a child head count sheet for field trips.

Tip | Attendance records should be stored in a secure place, such as a locked closet or file cabinet.

While there isn't a standard form for creating an attendance sheet, yours should contain the following information:

- The current date or, if your attendance will be recorded on a weekly basis, "Week of _____."

- The names of all of the children in your care.

- Space to write in the time at arrival and pickup.

- Space for the parent's or guardian's signature at arrival and at pickup.

Sunny Skies Child Care Attendance Sheet   **Date:**

Child's Name	Arrival Time	Signature	Pickup Time	Signature

Children's Developmental Records

There is no set format for recording information about a child. You may create your own documentation form, or you may use index cards or a notebook. Documentation can be done throughout the day. You may want to take notes on a child's developmental milestones or on a specific behavior to determine if there is a pattern that needs to be addressed. These notes, for example, may help you determine if a child is biting due to a language barrier or because she needs an adjustment to her sleep schedule.

Most documentation involves writing the child's first name, age, date, time, and location (play area). You want to write factual information and observations that will be easily interpreted when read by a third party. Documentation can also involve taking notes on positive behaviors, teachable moments, or play. These notes can help you plan lessons and activities that will interest the children. Normally, to protect the confidentiality of children, most caregivers use only the child's first name or use child A or child B if the document will be shared with someone other than the parent or guardian. For more on documentation, see chapter 10.

Menus

Place all of your weekly or monthly menus in a filing system that you can rotate. A binder can be helpful for keeping track of meal favorites and recipes. If you participate in the Child and Adult Care Food Program (CACFP), you are required to keep up-to-date records of attendance and all meals served. You may also want to take advantage of the online Food Program software that is offered through your local CACFP. For more information on these forms and programs, see chapter 14.

Other Records

There are various forms that you will need as your business develops, such as field trip permission forms, photo release forms, fire and tornado drill records, inspection records, training certificates, and other documentation. Create a file to maintain these records as the need arises.

Field Trip Permission Forms
Field trip permission forms should be kept on the premises. The form should have the name, date, and location of the trip along with the cost and transportation method. In addition, each child should have a permission slip signed by his or her parent or guardian. For more information on this topic, see chapter 15.

Photo Release Forms
Photo release forms provide permission for you to use children's photos in your literature highlighting your child care program. More information regarding photo release forms is in chapter 9.

Monthly Fire and Tornado Drills
Keep a log of monthly drills that includes the date and the children in attendance. For fire drills, add information about which exit you used and the time spent evacuating. For more information on drills and other safety issues, see chapter 11.

CPR and First Aid Training

Place your certificates and those of your employees in a file for safekeeping. For more information on safety issues, see chapter 11.

Professional Development Training

Place all of your child care conference, workshop, or college certificates together in a file as a record of training. For more information on training options, see chapter 16.

Furnace Inspection Log

Maintain a file of furnace inspections as needed.

Outdoor Equipment Inspections

Keep track of your annual, semiannual, or monthly equipment inspections for safety purposes for such things as swings, climbers, and slides. For more information on outdoor equipment, see chapter 12.

Maintenance and Warranties

Maintain a record of the scheduled maintenance on your home, such as your landscaping or snow removal, and applications of pesticides and exterminations, and document the warranties on your equipment.

Legal Documents

These documents, such as for your business bank accounts, business credit accounts, and insurance documents, should be filed in a fireproof and waterproof safe or file cabinet.

Assistant Caregivers

You should keep a file on each employee that includes each caregiver's contact information, criminal clearance record, physical and Tuberculosis (TB) forms, and CPR and first aid certificates. You may also place evaluation forms for your assistant caregivers in this file.

Payroll Records

It is important to develop some type of payroll system for your assistant caregivers.

If you have fewer than five employees, it may be a good idea to complete payroll yourself to reduce expenses. You may complete payroll manually or purchase a payroll software product. If you decide to perform payroll manually, you can find information to assist you on the IRS Web site at www.irs.gov.

Maintain Your Record-Keeping System

Maintaining your record-keeping system involves updating documents, shredding old documents, and adding new files as families come and go. Accurate record keeping can save you time by eliminating the need to search for documents. With practice, you will become more organized and effective in your business, saving time and money in the long run.

7

Budgeting

You have decided to care for life's most precious asset—children. While caring for children, you will also be engaged in the business of child care. The business portion sometimes gets neglected because it doesn't fit well with your passion for children. However, the business aspects of child care are as important to your success as providing quality care. Ideally, you want to maintain a profitable child care program and be recognized as a professional in the early childhood field. You can achieve this goal by maintaining a budget, which will help you keep track of your income, expenses, and profits.

Separate Personal and Business Expenses

Maintaining separate checking accounts for personal and business expenses is much easier than having to remember which bills were for child care and which were for personal use. Having separate checking accounts allows you to budget for your child care items and monitor expenses. It also reduces your paper trail, which simplifies expense records in the event you get audited by the IRS. If you decide to use one checking account for both personal and business purchases, jot a note on the receipt or in your check register to record whether the purchase was for business or personal use. If you pay by credit card or cash, make a note on the receipt just as you would for a check.

In addition to using the tips about estimating and tracking your expenses and income, you may want to hire an accountant to assist with the budgeting and tax portions of your child care business. Be sure that your accountant has experience working with family child care businesses. Finally, keep accurate records by staying organized. Maintaining proper documentation and knowing where to find pertinent items will reduce your stress and make you an effective manager.

Set Up a Budget

Setting up a budget can be a simple process that evolves over time. Initially, you estimate how much your total income and expenses will be. When you reach full

---

Family Child Care Business Planning Guide

Blank Budget Form

Income

Income from parents

Infants $_____/week x _____ weeks x _____ children	$_____
Toddlers $_____/week x _____ weeks x _____ children	$_____
Preschoolers $_____/week x _____ weeks x _____ children	$_____
Total	$_____

Program fees

Registration fees $_____ per child x _____ children	$_____

Food Program income[a]

$_____ per child per day x 5 days/week	
x _____ weeks x _____ children	$_____

Gross income	$_____

Income reductions[b]

Partial enrollment reduction (20%)	$_____
State subsidy program clients (5%)	$_____
Missed payments (2%)	$_____
Provider sick days (2%)	$_____
Total	$_____

Net income	$_____

Expenses

Business supplies

Children's supplies	$_____
Food	$_____
Toys	$_____
Household supplies	$_____
Other supplies (such as for special field trips)	$_____
Total	$_____

Other business expenses

Professional development	$_____
Advertising	$_____
Vehicle[c]	$_____
Depreciation of household items (furniture, appliances, etc.)	$_____
Business liability insurance	$_____
Office expenses	$_____
Repairs of toys, furniture, and equipment	$_____
Total	$_____

Home expenses[d]

Property tax	$_____
Mortgage interest	$_____
Utilities	$_____
Home repairs	$_____
Homeowners insurance	$_____
Business property insurance	$_____
Home depreciation or rent	$_____
Total	$_____

Blank Budget Form *(continued)*

Business loan (for start-up expenses)

Repayment of principal	$_____	
Loan interest	$_____	
Total		$_____

Other expenses

Employees	$_____	
Total		$_____

Total expenses	$_____
Net profit before taxes and retirement contribution[e] (net income – total expenses)	$_____

Retirement contribution	$_____

Net profit after retirement contribution[f]	$_____

Taxes

Social Security taxes[g]	$_____
Federal income taxes[h]	$_____
State income taxes[i]	$_____
Total	$_____

Net profit after taxes (net profit before retirement – total taxes)	$_____
Cash on hand at the end of the year (net profit after taxes – retirement contribution)	$_____

a. Project your reimbursements for the upcoming year based on the current rate that applies to your program.

b. Because these reductions are percentages of gross income, note that they reduce both parent fees and Food Program income.

c. For this number, multiply your business mileage by the current IRS mileage reimbursement rate.

d. For the numbers in this section, multiply your actual home expenses by your Time-Space percentage. If you aren't sure what your Time-Space percentage will be, you can use 40% as a ballpark estimate.

e. Use this number to calculate your Social Security taxes.

f. Use this number to calculate your income taxes.

g. If your net profit before taxes is greater than $400, enter 15.3% of that total on this line; otherwise, enter 0.

h. Consult a tax professional for the amount that you should budget for federal income tax.

i. Consult a tax professional for the amount that you should budget for state income tax.

Family Child Care Business Planning Guide by Tom Copeland, JD. Copyright © 2009 by Tom Copeland. Reprinted with permission from Redleaf Press. You can download a copy of this budget form from the Redleaf Press Web site at www.redleafpress.org. Enter "Business Planning Guide" into the search field and follow the links.

enrollment, you can create a more precise budget. A monthly budget for a family child care business might look similar to the one above, continued from page 35.

Project Your Income

Projected income statements are used to show the financial viability of your child care business. These statements can be submitted as the monthly, quarterly, or annually projected income you set up in your business plan (see chapter 2). Initially, these statements will show a loss because of start-up expenses, but then will gradually show a profit as you receive more children into your program. A projected income statement for a family child care might look similar to the one on page 37.

Cash Flow Projection	JAN	FEB	MAR	APR	MAY	JUN	JUL	AUG	SEP	OCT	NOV	DEC	Total
Number of weeks in month													
Income (cash inflows)													
Cash on hand													
Infant @ $175/week													
Toddler @ $145/week													
Toddler @ $145/week													
Preschooler @ $125/week													
Preschooler @ $125/week													
Preschooler @ $125/week													
Registration fees													
Food Program reimbursements													
Holding fees													
Grant													
Total													
Expenses (cash outflows)													
Advertising													
Vehicle expenses													
Business liability insurance													
Disability income insurance													
Loan interest													
Office expenses													
Repairs													
Children's supplies													
Food													
Toys													
Household supplies													
Field trips													
Professional development													
Property taxes													
Mortgage payment													
Utilities													
Homeowners insurance													
Repairs													
Business property insurance													
Estimated taxes													
Retirement contribution													
Total													
Net profit (income − expenses)													
Personal draw													
Cash on hand (cash inflows − cash outflows)													

Determine Expenses

You will have many expenses that arise from opening your family child care business. Keeping track of your dollars is important and involves a series of checks and balances. Your goal is to maintain a budget that makes your business profitable. An obvious way to ensure a profit at the end of the year is to keep your expenses lower than your income. As straightforward as that sounds, it is not an easy task. There are many things that eat away at your income. Here is a brief list of some of your major expenses:

- lease or mortgage

- utilities

- food

- taxes

- insurance

- supplies

- equipment

- toys

In addition to these expenses, there are often little items you'll find to purchase for your children that weren't in the budget. I call these items *nibblers* because they nibble away at your bottom line. Nibblers can erase any profit you think you should have at the end of each month. For example, you may go to buy supplies at your local craft store and see a great craft activity on display, which adds another twenty dollars to your craft store bill. Or while on a walk with the children in the neighborhood, you spot a cute little table at a garage sale that would be just perfect in the toddler area. Most providers justify nibblers by saying, "I may need this later," "It's on sale," or "This is a great deal, and I just can't pass it up." While it may be difficult to pass up a great bargain, you must remain focused. Set an income goal for your business and stick with it. It also helps to place nibblers into your budget. Set aside a small amount for nibbler items so you can purchase things that are not in the budget, but that will save money and add value to your program in the long term.

Keep Track of Income and Expenses

One of the simplest ways to effectively track your income and expenses is to expand your budget and record all of the income you receive each month. This income might come from tuition payments, state subsidy payments, Food Program reimbursements, or any other resources that bring money into your business. You also need to record your expenses. Initially you will have more expenses due to start-up costs, such as licensing fees, logo design, marketing, space preparation, initial banking fees, registering your business name, toy and equipment purchases, and so on. Your other working expenses, such as taxes, insurance, advertising, and food, will enter the picture as soon as you open your doors for child care.

To help track and record expenses, get a receipt or invoice for everything you purchase for your business and make a small note in your journal, or write a notation on the receipt with a pen, regarding the purchase. Keep the receipts in a file and record the expenses in your expanded budget. I've noticed that the receipts I typically receive at the supermarkets are printed on special paper with ink that smears and virtually vanishes over time. To preserve your receipts, you may want to invest in a small copier or scanner to duplicate your receipts before you file them.

Keeping track of expenses is probably one of the most cumbersome tasks for caregivers. You have many expenses and line items to document and track to ensure the success of your child care business. Fortunately, there are software programs customized to handle this time-consuming task. These programs minimize the time away from the children, and I highly recommend utilizing one. Research the product offerings and select a program that fits your budget and will give you maximum results. My favorites include ProCare, available at www.procaresoftware.com, Childcare Manager, available at www.childcaremanager.com, DayCare Information Systems Pro, available at www.sdssoftwaresolutions.com, Minute

Menu, available at www.minutemenu.com, and EZCare2, available at www.ezcare2.com. *The Redleaf Calendar-Keeper* is another valuable tool, available at www.redleafpress.org.

Additional Resources

I highly recommend you download or call to request a copy of IRS Publication 583 Starting a Business and Keeping Records. This document provides instructions on recording expenses and keeping records. In addition to Publication 583, you may want to purchase the *Family Child Care Record-Keeping Guide* by Tom Copeland, available at www.redleafpress.org. This book offers information on how to properly prepare documents and organize your records as well as provides a more detailed look at tracking income and expenses.

8

Interviewing Families

Interviewing families is one of the most important aspects of your business because it is your opportunity to show potential families your child care program. Families will be closely evaluating your personal characteristics, responses to their questions, and the learning environments you have created. It may be best to set aside a time after closing for the initial interview, then invite the family to return during child care hours to observe your interactions with the children. Remember to remain calm and allow families to see your passion as a family child care provider.

Plan to Receive Inquiry Calls

When potential families call, be prepared to give a summary of your services. Provide enough information to pique their interest in the services you offer; for example, "I open at 5:30 AM and provide a preschool curriculum. In addition, I offer transportation as well as dance and music lessons." Encourage callers to set an appointment to continue the discussion and tour your facility. Remember, your primary job is to take care of the children. Do not spend too much time on the telephone.

Prepare to Meet Potential Families

A potential family has called to inquire about your services, and they will visit tomorrow. What should you do to prepare?

- It is imperative that you look and sound professional when meeting a family for the first time. First impressions are lasting impressions. Present yourself in a relaxed yet professional manner. Remember, this meeting could lead to a long-term business relationship.

- Prior to meeting a family, check that your home is clean and free of unpleasant odors. I review my home for safety and clean or remove anything that is an eyesore.

- I also ensure that my clothing or smock is clean, so that I look refreshed and feel energetic about our first meeting. Typically, I'd wear business casual attire, such as slacks and a blouse or sweater. Your appearance communicates your professionalism and expertise to families.

- Prepare for the interview by having necessary paperwork ready, such as application and registration forms, a child information sheet, family handbook, immunization forms, and so on. See chapters 6 and 9 for more information about paperwork.

- Be prepared for different ages of children. For example, if you are expecting a family with a toddler, you may want to have a table or area to display items appropriate for the child's growth and development. See the next section for additional ideas about display tables.

Display Tables

A display table shows potential families a sample of developmentally appropriate activities their children can engage in while in your care.

- Display a few items appropriate for the child's age and developmental level. Include stimulating and open-ended materials that enhance children's cognitive, creative, physical, language, and social skills. Do not overcrowd the table. For infants, a display table could have soft books, picture books, textured toys and balls, different types of rattles, and a mat or large blanket for tummy-time activities. In addition to the display table, I set a calming, soothing tone for the infant area by playing soft classical or lullaby music and using low-wattage lighting or a lamp. The toddler table could hold large, lightweight cushion blocks, cars and trucks, picture books, knob puzzles, dolls, and homemade toys. The preschool table could have a matching game, puzzles, repetitive books, science materials, manipulatives, costumes, and musical instruments.

- Demonstrate how the materials are used and explain the skills that children develop. For example, you can explain that a knob puzzle is great for a child's small hands to grasp. "By grasping the knobs, the child is developing small-muscle skills. When the child lifts a puzzle piece, he sees the same picture underneath, which enhances his thinking and reasoning skills. He will be able to decide where each piece fits. Matching picture cards helps build language skills and word recognition. The cards are shared with other toddlers, which helps develop socialization and play skills."

- The table should include a mix of store bought and handmade materials. Displaying handmade materials shows your uniqueness and creativity in developing your program.

- If you decide not to use a display table, be sure to point out materials specific to a potential family's child's needs during a tour of your center and explain how the materials will benefit their child's development.

Prepare Questions

Take time to prepare questions to gather information you would like to know about a prospective family, which will help you adequately prepare for the enrollment of a child into your program. The following are a few questions I often ask during my first meeting with a family. Please feel free to add questions you think are helpful and important in making sound decisions about enrollment.

What are your expectations of me as your child's caregiver?

This question will help you identify areas that you can accommodate. You'll want to address these during the tour. If there is something that you cannot provide, such as transportation, extended hours, or something that you are just not comfortable with, you need to tell the family up front. I often hear providers complain about parents who request homework assignments or ask the provider to dress the child in the morning or take a child to a doctor's appointment. We are not nannies, we are child care providers. We want to accommodate families' requests without putting unrealistic activities on our long to-do list.

This is also a time for parents to inform you if their child has a disability. Many family child care providers have inclusive child care where children with special needs are accommodated. The parents and caregivers work together to ensure a quality environment for all of the children in care. Become familiar with the Americans with Disabilities Act (ADA) and Title III. This information will help you determine if you can *reasonably accommodate* a child with special needs. The Web site for the ADA is www.ada.gov. You can select "Commonly Asked Questions About Child Care Centers and the ADA" for more information.

Does Blake have any dietary restrictions or preferences?

This is an opportunity for parents to inform you of allergies as well as food likes and dislikes. Yes, some children are picky eaters, but I have found that they eat more types of foods when meals are served family style. See chapter 14 for more information.

What disciplinary methods do you practice at home?

You want to understand how the child is disciplined for inappropriate conduct because you may have to modify your discipline methods to match the parents' style. This may rarely happen. Most children are okay with redirection, choices, and proper guidance by the caregiver.

What kinds of activities does Blake enjoy most? Least?

This information will help you make a smooth transition for the child.

Give a Tour

Give potential families a tour to show off your facility. Please don't assume that parents know everything about family child care. You will want to explain your learning environments as well as your procedures. Take this opportunity to carefully listen to the family's needs. The first tour is very important. You may have this child in your care for five or more years depending on the age of the child and the family's child care needs. Consider the following advice when giving a family a tour.

- During the tour, direct the family's attention to your license display. Inform them of your credentials and the credentials of your staff, if appropriate.

- Invite the parents to call you by your first name and ask permission to do the same. Addressing one another by first name is more informal and helps build a relationship with the family. See chapter 10 for more information.

- Use the display table to guide a discussion on developmentally appropriate practices used in your child care.

- Show the family all of your learning environments and explain their organization. See chapter 13 for more information on planning daily activities.

- Be sure to mention how often you clean and rotate your materials and equipment and check for safety hazards. Show the family the toileting and diaper-changing areas.

- Ensure that your own family is not distracting you during the interview. If they are home, introduce them to the prospective family and then direct the touring family to an area free of distractions.

- Be sure to use the child's name throughout the tour. Instead of saying, "Tell me about your child's favorite foods," you could say, "Barbara, what types of foods does Katie enjoy eating?" Or, if the child is old enough to answer, ask her directly.

- Make eye contact with the parents and the child during the tour. Bend at the knees to the child's eye level and introduce yourself.

- Remember, every child's temperament is different, and not every child will warm up to you at your first meeting. You should ask if it is okay to give the child a hug. The slow-to-warm-up child may need time in your home before any type of close contact can be made. You may play a game with the child or offer a toy, such as a puzzle or manipulative, that you both can use.

- Ask the parents' permission to hold their infant. Most parents would like you to make some type of contact with their child during the tour. Just don't over-do it.

*Tip | Just because a touring family has been referred to your program doesn't mean that you should relax during a tour. The family will look for the qualities the reference mentioned, plus they may have their own priorities.

Follow Up

After the tour, send a brief letter thanking the family for touring your facility. In the letter, make reference to something that you discussed or enclose a pamphlet or article about a topic that was mentioned during the tour, such as biting or toilet learning. Remember to check the letter for errors. Pay careful attention to the spelling of family members' names. You can put the letter on your business letterhead or a paper with nice graphics. A sample letter is below.

Sunny Skies Child Care
232 Wayward Lane
Brownstown, IN 47220
555-222-1234
childcare@sunnyskies.com

January 19, 2010

Mr. and Mrs. Terry Reynolds
23421 Castlet Court
Brownstown, IN 47220

Dear Terry and Michelle,

I would like to take this opportunity to thank you for touring Sunny Skies Child Care. It was a pleasure to meet you and Todd. As promised, I've enclosed an article about speech development that I think you will find helpful.

The early years of Todd's life are critical years for learning. He needs a positive environment that will enhance his social, physical, cognitive, creative, and language development. Sunny Skies Child Care offers such an environment. We would love to have Todd join us as he explores creative ways of learning these critical components for his future. If you have any questions, please e-mail, call, or stop by. I look forward to hearing from you soon.

Sincerely,

Chamayne N. Green,
Director

Provide References

If a family likes your program, but is still unsure about enrolling their child, offer to have current or former families available for a reference. You may need references to win over a family if you are a new caregiver, have recently relocated, or have a higher priced service compared to other child care programs in your area. Be sure to request permission prior to listing someone's name as a reference.

*Tip | Save thank-you letters and cards from former families showing their appreciation for your services. Have them readily available to help assure parents about the quality of care you provide. Having a portfolio of photos and letters available during a tour serves as an indicator of great service.

Write a Welcome Letter

When a family decides to enroll their child, send them a welcome letter and a copy of your family handbook to read. In the letter, ask the parents to sign and return the parent agreement prior to the child's first day. The welcome letter should include a statement of thanks for selecting your child care program, a statement about the benefits of enrolling their child, and a checklist of items needed prior to the first day. See chapter 9 for information about handbooks. Here is an example of a welcome letter.

Sunny Skies Child Care
232 Wayward Lane
Brownstown, IN 47220
555-222-1234
childcare@sunnyskies.com

January 25, 2010

Mr. and Mrs. Terry Reynolds
23421 Castlet Court
Brownstown, IN 47220

Dear Terry and Michelle,

We are excited that you chose Sunny Skies Child Care to help enhance Todd's early development! We are expecting Todd to join the Sunny Skies Child Care family on February 1. Enclosed is our family handbook and the parent agreement. Please read the handbook and call or e-mail me if you have any questions. Please sign and return the parent agreement prior to Todd's first day. We also need the following items on or before Todd's first day:

· registration forms (enclosed)
· Food Program registration form
· a change of clothing labeled with his name
· diapers
· tuition payment
· security deposit

To help make Todd's first day easier, please also bring a photograph of your family and a blanket, stuffed animal, or toy that Todd will know from home.

Sincerely,

Chamayne N. Green,
Director

9

Developing a Family Handbook

Every family child care business owner should create a family handbook. A family handbook details your policies and procedures and is used to explain your expectations and the types of services you offer to prospective families. Your family handbook should also serve as a welcome, or orientation, packet for families whose children enter your care. Once you determine that a family is ready to enroll their child, give them a copy of the family handbook to review and a copy of the parent agreement to sign and return, preferably before their child care begins.

Guidelines and Policies

A family handbook serves as part of the professional relationship between you and the families you serve. Please take steps to ensure that the policies and procedures you implement are fair and reasonable. The content of your handbook should be friendly and professional. If you have many policies, outline and number them to make the handbook more accessible. A table of contents may also be helpful.

Your family handbook should also have an attached parent agreement, or contract, for families to sign. This document confirms that the family agrees with the policies set forth in the handbook and will abide by the rules and procedures outlined in it. The family handbook can be used as a legal document, so please have an attorney review it before you begin using it.

Create Your Family Handbook

Family handbooks can be created to your specifications. Each family handbook is unique because each child care program has its own policies and procedures. The appearance of your handbook can also be personalized. You may want your name and logo on the front cover along with pictures of the children in your program. Be creative! Depending on the number of policies you want to include, your handbook can be as few as four pages or as many as twenty pages. Keep in mind that you want parents to read each policy. The text should be concise and easy to understand. Use simple wording and examples that will help explain your reasoning. Here are some tips to keep in mind when writing your family handbook:

- Use short, direct sentences and phrases.
- Include a clause or statement allowing you the right to make changes if necessary, usually with a thirty- or sixty-day notice.
- Include a clause stating that the handbook is the property of your child care organization and should not be shared without your consent.
- Have your handbook proofread for spelling, grammar, and punctuation errors.
- Print your handbook on high-quality paper.
- Take notes throughout the year regarding changes you'd like to make to your handbook and review the proposed changes before each new printing.
- Update your handbook each year, even if you don't change anything except the date.

Sample Handbook

Family handbooks have standard policies to protect you and the families enrolled in your program. The following is a list of sample policies and sample text that may be included in your family handbook. You may have additional policies that are not outlined within this sample handbook.

Sunny Skies Child Care

Welcome to Sunny Skies Child Care. I am delighted that you chose to become part of the Sunny Skies family. This family handbook will guide you through our policies and procedures to help make your transition easier. I created this handbook to build a mutual agreement of program expectations for both myself and the families in my program. Please read over the entire handbook and contact me if you have any questions or concerns.

Mission Statement
Sunny Skies Child Care's mission is to provide a quality early childhood environment for young children and families.

Philosophy Statement
My philosophy is that every child should have a solid foundation in the early years of his or her life. I believe in developing the whole child. I understand the special needs of young children and provide an inclusive environment for them. I provide positive interactions that enhance each child's social, cognitive, creative, physical, and language development.

Nondiscrimination Policy
Sunny Skies Child Care has a policy that prohibits discrimination based on race, color, religion, national origin, gender, or disability.

Enrollment/Admission Requirements
Sunny Skies enrollment is year round. The enrollment is open for children six months to seven years old. We accept full-time children only. Full-time care consists of nine-and-a-half hours of care each day.

Confidentiality
The staff of Sunny Skies Child Care respects your right to privacy. We will not share any confidential information among staff or families without your permission or consent unless mandated by child care licensing regulations, other statutes, or by a court of law. Sunny Skies Child Care is also obligated to protect children's privacy, which includes withholding the names of children who may have been involved in incidents that occur in our program.

Hours of Operation

Our hours of operation are 6:00 AM to 6:00 PM Monday through Friday. Your child will be allowed nine-and-a-half hours of care each day.

Deposits

A deposit of fifty dollars is required to hold your child's space in the Sunny Skies program. This fee is nonrefundable and will be used as part of the administrative expenses for enrollment. A two-week payment is due at the beginning of care. This payment will serve as the first and last tuition payment for each child enrolled.

Tuition and Fees

Tuition payments are made in advance of the services rendered. Normally, you can submit payment on the Friday before or the Monday morning of the week care will begin. If you choose to make monthly or semimonthly payments, tuition will be due by the beginning of each month or in two-week intervals. To continue offering a quality program, we must impose a late-payment fee to those who miss their scheduled tuition payments. A forty dollar late-payment fee will be added to any tuition payments not made by the due date.

If you are late picking your child up on any given day, the standard late fee of twenty dollars per half hour or any fraction thereof will be imposed. Late pickup fees are collected the day after the fee was incurred.

There may be times when you will need to make temporary changes to your child care schedule by extending your child's normal hours in the morning or at the end of the day. The overtime rate for this temporary change is ten dollars per one-half hour or a fraction thereof for the extended time. It is imperative that you give advance notice when you need to extend your scheduled child care.

Types of Payments

Sunny Skies Child Care accepts payments made by cash, check, money order, and electronic debit. Returned checks will incur a thirty-five dollar fee in addition to any late-payment fees, and afterward you will be required to make cash payments.

Sunny Skies Child Care ☼ 2

Absences

We prepare many activities for each child in our care, and we miss your child when he or she is not here. Please contact Sunny Skies Child Care if your child is going to be absent for any reason. There are no tuition deductions for absences unless the child has been ill. Please refer to our illness policy regarding absences.

Reporting a Schedule Change

Please call or tell us in person ahead of time if

1. your child will not be attending.
2. your child will be more than thirty minutes late.
3. you are going to be late picking up your child.
4. someone other than you will be picking up your child.
5. your child is sick and you are unsure whether he or she should attend.
6. your child will leave early because of a medical or dental appointment.

Children's Vacations

Each family is allowed a one-week vacation. You are not required to pay tuition for this week. The vacation time may only be taken as a whole week and not divided into days. A two-week advance notice is required before vacation can be deducted from tuition.

> ***Tip** It is optional to offer vacation time for children. One week of unpaid vacation for each child can be a huge reduction in income for a family child care provider.

Provider's Vacations

> ***Tip** This can be paid or unpaid time for you. You may want to provide alternative care choices during this time.

While we understand that you need year-round care, it is important for the staff of Sunny Skies to take time off to relax in order to maintain a quality child care environment. You will receive a two-month notice of any vacation time for our staff.

Conference Days

Throughout the course of the year, our staff members will attend child care conferences and training sessions to improve the quality of care we provide and to meet state licensing training mandates. The majority of conferences are held in the evenings and on the weekends. However, it is possible that our child care home may close so that we can attend a conference. We will try to arrange to have a substitute available, but this is not always possible. Advance notice will be given for those days. Full tuition is due for conference days.

> ***Tip** You may decide not to take time off during business hours to attend a conference or not charge your families for conference time. This decision is yours.

3 ☼ Sunny Skies Child Care

Emergency Closings

Sunny Skies reserves the right to close due to a provider's inability to care for the children because of her own illness, or the illness of an immediate family member, that may be contagious and infect the children. We also reserve the right to close in an emergency due to a funeral, jury duty, and so on. In the event of an emergency closing, Sunny Skies will attempt to find alternative child care arrangements for the families enrolled.

> ***Tip** This type of closing gives you an opportunity to care for yourself or your family when ill. Depending on the illness or circumstance you may really need personal time off, so please consider adding this type of clause to your family handbook.

Business Interruption

Sunny Skies Child Care may be closed due to weather conditions, loss of electricity, an unexpected repair to the child care space, communicable disease outbreaks, and so on. In the event that the child care is closed for more than two days, you are not required to make tuition payments. In the event of a business interruption, Sunny Skies will attempt to find alternative child care arrangements for the families enrolled.

> ***Tip** This is also an optional clause. I have seen a power outage cause a child care home to close, and the provider was unsure about charging tuition during this time. It may be possible to get your insurance to help cover the loss of business during interruptions. Please check with your insurance company regarding these types of business losses.

Sick Child Policy

It is absolutely imperative for the safety and protection of all the children and staff that you let us know of any medical conditions that your child may have, with the exception of conditions protected under the Americans with Disabilities Act (ADA). It is the responsibility of Sunny Skies Child Care to provide a safe and healthy environment for all of the children enrolled in our program. **Immunizations must be kept up to date unless you have submitted an immunization waiver.** Please contact Sunny Skies if your child is ill and will not be attending care. Children should be kept home if they have an unexplained rash, ring worm, pink eye, or any symptoms of contagious illnesses. Your child should also be kept home if he or she has a fever above 100.4 degrees Fahrenheit, is vomiting, or has diarrhea (loose stools).

You will be contacted if your child has any of the symptoms listed above while in our care. We will do our best to give him or her tender loving care until you arrive. Your child may need to be isolated, depending on the symptoms, to reduce the spread of illness to other children. Please treat your child's illness as an emergency and pick your child up as soon as possible. For specific illnesses, we may require a doctor's note for clearance to resume care. You will not be required to pay tuition if your child misses more than three days in a week due to illness. The tuition will be prorated for the days he or she was in care. Tuition is also not required if your child is hospitalized or has a surgical procedure.

Medication Policy

Sunny Skies Child Care will only dispense over-the-counter and pre-scribed medication that is accompanied by a written permission form. All medication must have the proper dosage listed and be in the origi-nal, labeled containers. We will follow the dosage information given on the labeled items. For example, if the label states that children under the age of six should not take this medication, and your child is under the age of six, then we will not dispense the medication to your child. Prescribed medication must have your child's name and the proper dosage amount on the label. For the security of your child, Sunny Skies requests that you provide a dosing cup or syringe with your child's prescriptions.

Photo Releases

Sunny Skies enjoys taking pictures of the children to display in our child care setting. At times we may use these pictures on our flyers or other advertisements and in our family handbook or in articles about our child care. We request written permission to use your child's pictures for the purposes listed above. We will not sell or share your child's pic-tures to any third-party entities. If you agree to provide this permission, please complete the consent form provided at the back of this handbook.

Discipline

Sunny Skies Child Care is required by law to adhere to state regulations regarding disciplining a child. All of the following methods of handling children are prohibited:

- restricting a child's movement by binding or tying
- withholding necessary food, rest, or toilet use
- confining a child in an area, such as in a closet or locked room
- humiliating, threatening, or yelling at a child by a staff member

Sunny Skies will use positive discipline techniques that will teach your child how to correct inappropriate behavior. Children will be given a brief explanation of their behavior and how it affects other children and themselves and then redirected to another activity. We will contact you if the behavior persists or causes concern. If the behavior is consistent, a conference will be set up to determine the best steps for handling the behavior.

Biting Policy

Sunny Skies understands the developmental needs of toddlers. We know that biting under the age of three is a part of children's normal development. Biting does occur in a variety of child care settings for many reasons, including lack of verbal skills, teething, hunger, and frustration. We will use our training and expertise to reduce biting in our program. If a child has been bitten, we will use proper first aid treatment and notify the parent. It's important that both the child who bites and the child who has been bitten receive attention and understanding. Parents of both children will be contacted, and the children's names will remain confidential. If your child bites and the behavior is persistent and causing harm to other children, you may have to seek alternate care for your child. However, this would only be requested after Sunny Skies and your family have exhausted all resources, including shadowing the child and seeking outside assistance.

> ***Tip** A great resource for biting is the book *No Biting: Policy and Practice for Toddler Programs* by Gretchen Kinnell available from Redleaf Press.

Food

Sunny Skies provides nutritious meals and snacks to all the children in our care. We provide a monthly menu, and your child will receive breakfast, lunch, and an afternoon snack. Please inform us of any food allergies that your child may have. Sunny Skies requests that you label all formula and breast milk with your child's name and the date.

Clothing

Sunny Skies has a play-based environment; therefore, we would like your child to be dressed in play clothing. We are not responsible for damage, stains, or tears to your child's clothing. Please do not allow your child to wear necklaces, rings, or bracelets that can become lost or present a choking hazard to them or other children. Please bring an extra set of clothing that is appropriate for the weather conditions.

Sunny Skies Child Care ☼ 6

Supplies

Please bring the following supplies for your child's first day. Be sure to label everything with your child's name.

Infants and Toddlers

- a complete change of clothing, including socks
- a package of diapers
- a day's supply of bottles

Preschoolers

- a complete change of clothing, including socks

Smoking

Smoking is prohibited both during and after hours of operation to ensure the health and safety of your child.

Parking

You may park in the driveway or on the street. As a courtesy to my neighbors, please do not blow your car horn or play loud music.

Hiring of Staff by Parents

There may be times when you need child care after hours. Sunny Skies will not be held responsible for the care of your children by any employees after the employee's normal working hours or off the premises of Sunny Skies Child Care.

Parent Conduct

It is important to maintain a professional relationship with the families of Sunny Skies Child Care. For the safety of the children, we request that you refrain from any unprofessional conduct while at our facility. Such unprofessional conduct would include

- verbal or physical abuse of a child
- profanity
- threats to or harassment of staff, children, or other adults
- violent acts
- possessing drugs or alcohol on the premises

These actions may result in termination of the parent-caregiver agreement from Sunny Skies Child Care and contact of the local police agency.

Field Trips

Sunny Skies Child Care offers field trips throughout the year, and we request that parents help chaperone the field trips. You will receive a field trip permission form that details the trip and the costs. We transport children on our field trips using a local transportation company. If you decide not to allow your child to attend a field trip, you will be responsible for making alternative care arrangements at your expense. Field trip days are included in the tuition fees regardless of whether the child attends the field trip.

> ***Tip** Field trips are optional, but they are great experiences! Please read chapter 15 for more information.

Terminating Enrollment

Sunny Skies Child Care has the right to terminate the child care agreement without notice for the following reasons or circumstances:

- consistently harmful behavior
- uncontrollable behavior
- excessive late pickups
- excessive late payments
- nonpayment
- excessive absences

Parent Participation

Sunny Skies Child Care welcomes you to volunteer while your child is in our care. You will be required to complete a criminal background check prior to your participation.

Right to Change a Policy

Sunny Skies Child Care reserves the right to add, delete, modify, or amend the policies set forth therein upon sixty days written notice.

Sunny Skies Child Care ☼ 8

Statement of Receipt/Parent Agreement

I/WE _____ have received and read the policies
and procedures of Sunny Skies Child Care. I/WE understand and agree
to comply with the information set forth therein.

Parent/Guardian Signature _____

Date _____

Parent/Guardian Signature _____

Date _____

Consent Form

Sunny Skies Child Care has my permission to use
(child's name) _____ photos for family
handbooks, advertising, and literature. I understand that the photos
will not be sold, exchanged, transferred, or used publicly for monetary
gain or value.

Parent/Guardian Signature _____

Date _____

10

Building Relationships with Families

Building healthy relationships with families is important to the development of the children in your child care program. A healthy relationship builds trust and confidence so the child will have a quality home-school connection. There are many ways to support a positive relationship with parents, and this section will discuss several of them.

Partner with Parents

Let families know that, as a caregiver, your job is to support them in their efforts to raise their children. Inform parents that they are partnering with you to help enhance their child's learning and development. The partnership involves collaboration, consistency, and a commitment to working toward the common goal of the care and development of their child. Explain how you can help lay a solid foundation of learning that will affect their children for the rest of their lives.

Parents are often very uneasy the first time they leave their child in a new setting. We want to assure parents that their child is receiving the highest quality of care while they are away. During your first meeting, try to make a good first impression on parents. Assure them that you are the best person to care for their child. Inform them about why you are in the child care business, and let your passion for children shine through by showing affection for their child, having a warm smile, and being professional. Let parents know about your goals and philosophy as well as your expectations. Listen to their ideas about parenting and about how you can assist them in their efforts. It is important not only to build trust with the children, but also to build trust with the parents.

Document Children's Development

Documentation may be used to help you recall and share with parents their child's developmental milestones. Documentation is also helpful when you want to record a pattern of behavior or changes to a child's disposition. Documenting the behavior of a child who is going through a biting phase, for example, may help you determine a pattern of when that child will most likely bite. You can also use documentation to recall a conversation between you and the parent or to record critical information a child may share with you regarding abuse or neglect. For more information, see chapter 6.

Hold Family Conferences

Be sure to set aside time throughout the year to meet one-on-one with each family. Family conferences give you and the parents a chance to voice concerns, learn more about a child's development, and build a strong relationship. Prior to the conference, prepare a checklist of things you want to accomplish. Always present positive information about the child first, then discuss your concerns. Use documentation (see the previous paragraph) to support the information you present. Have resources available and/or possible solutions ready. Always end your meeting with a positive tone, by telling a funny story about the child, sharing a wonderful photo, or reiterating your appreciation of having their child in your child care program.

Communicate Effectively

Effective communication is key to building healthy relationships with families. There are three types of communication you can use to become an effective communicator with families—verbal, nonverbal, and written. Before we take a look at each type, remember that communication is a two-way street. You must effectively listen to your families' concerns and questions as well.

Verbal Communication

Verbal communication begins as soon as a parent calls to inquire about prices or availability. You can help put a parent at ease by learning how to respond in a tone and manner that will assure the parent that you are a good choice for their child's care. When communicating with parents, remain positive and upbeat. Be sure to greet adults and siblings during drop-off and pickup. This is when most relationship building will occur.

Think about the following sentences. How would they affect parents? Might they lead to further discussion between you and the parents? What else can you say to build healthy relationships?

- "Good Morning Ms. Jones. How are you and Sarah today?"

- "I noticed that Mihir didn't eat much of his lunch yesterday. How was dinner-time last night?"

- "We have a great report to give you today. Cally put on her shoes by herself!"

- "We're here to help with the toilet-learning process, so please inform us when you decide it's time for Nadia to start."

- "Good-bye, have a great evening. Be sure to ask Max all about his painting activity."

The following are a few additional tips for verbal communication:

- Use clear, concise speech.

- Speak to adults using lay terms. Try to avoid educational terms that may be unfamiliar or confusing.

- Try to keep conversations informal so parents will feel relaxed. Introducing yourself by your first name and requesting to address them by their first name usually helps with this effort.

Nonverbal Communication

As a caregiver, you want to make sure that your nonverbal communication is in sync with your verbal communication. When speaking to parents

- have a warm smile;

- maintain eye contact unless cultural traditions prohibit it;

- use open hand gestures rather than pointing to reduce the possibility of being seen as insensitive of another culture;

- avoid folding your arms;

- use good posture;

- be attentive.

Written Communication

There are many tools to aid written communication with families. Some of the most common include newsletters, daily reports, and accident reports. When sending written communication home for parents, be sure to check for spelling and grammatical errors.

Newsletters are typically a weekly or monthly written communication tool used to inform families of themes or lessons plans, field trips, birthdays, special events, and anything else that may be important to share. They are usually one page and feature many short topics. Be creative with your newsletter. You can use computer software to add graphics, change fonts, and even insert pictures.

May 2011

Sunny Skies Child Care

In-House Field Trip

We will be dancing and singing to the music of Kim's Place on Monday, May 10. Ms. Kim will bring a variety of instruments and activities for the children to enjoy. Please have all the children present by 10:00 AM. A special thank-you goes out to Ms. Judy King (Anthony's mom) for inviting Ms. Kim to Sunny Skies Child Care.

Theme of the Month

The theme for the month of May is "Exploring Insects." Our caterpillars will be arriving soon. We are waiting for stable weather. Please bring in any insects that will be safe for the children to explore. (Pictures are fine as well.)

Trike-A-Thon News

A special thank-you goes out to the parents and children of Sunny Skies Child Care for your generous contributions to our Trike-A-Thon. We were able to donate $235 to help the children at St. Jude's Research Hospital.

Fertilizers and Pesticides

Sunny Skies Child Care will be using Nature's Way to fertilize our lawn. Nature's Way products are all-natural and safe for children and pets once the fertilizer is dry. Children have not had any previous reactions to this fertilizer; please contact us if your child experiences an unexplained rash or illness. Pesticide bait traps will be used in and around the house to help us stay free of the spiders and ants that tend to invade during the warm months. These pesticides will be used after hours or on weekends and will not interfere with the child care areas.

Don't Forget!
Sunny Skies Is Closed for Memorial Day
We will be closed on Monday, May 31, in observance of Memorial Day.

Daily Reports provide parents with a quick update of their child's day. These notices are used especially to inform parents of the daily events of infants and preverbal toddlers. Many family child care providers also use these reports to give updates on a child who is new to the program, has special needs or separation anxiety, reaches a milestone, has a change in behavior, or needs special attention.

Toddler Daily Report

Parents, please complete this section.

Child's name _____

Today my child seemed
- ☐ Active as usual
- ☐ A bit fussy
- ☐ Other _____

Last night my child slept
- ☐ Soundly
- ☐ Restlessly

Today my child woke up at
_____ AM/PM

Today my child ate
- ☐ Breakfast before coming
- ☐ Nothing before coming

Today, please note for my child
- ☐ Diet changes _____
- ☐ Activities to avoid _____
- ☐ Medication _____
- ☐ Other _____
  _____

Parents, here is information on your child's day.

Today your child
- ☐ Showed curiosity and interest in surroundings
- ☐ Found own play area or activity
- ☐ Was happy and played well
- ☐ Enjoyed activities
- ☐ Needed more attention
- ☐ Was tired
- ☐ Did not participate much

Today your child ate
- ☐ All
- ☐ Most
- ☐ A little
- ☐ None

During naptime your child
- ☐ Slept
- ☐ Rested quietly
- ☐ Was restless

Today your child
- ☐ Wore diapers
- ☐ Wore underpants
- ☐ Used the potty
- ☐ Had a BM
- ☐ Toileting comments _____
  _____

Please bring
- ☐ Extra clothes
- ☐ Other _____
  _____

Comments
_____

Redleaf Easy Forms

Incident Reports should be completed and shared with parents any time a child has a small bump, scrape, or bruise. A more serious injury requires immediate parent or guardian notification. Your state licensing agency may have specific forms available for more serious injuries.

Child's Name	Date of Injury	Time of Injury	Describe What Happened	Type of Injury	Staff Witness	First Aid Treatment Given/ Administered By	Parent Signature

Injury Log — Week of _____

Redleaf Easy Forms

Encourage Parent Participation

Parents can bring a wealth of knowledge and diversity to your program, so invite them to volunteer. Most are happy to assist. Invite parents on a field trip (see page 103) or to speak to the children about their profession. Not all parents' schedules allow them to assist in your child care setting. Involve these adults by asking them to donate items or help set up a community event.

Give parents small responsibilities when they volunteer. Ask them to read stories, assist with an arts-and-crafts activity, or help supervise children during an outdoor water activity. You want to be sure that a parent has a criminal background check through your local police department or human services agency prior to volunteering. How do you even broach the subject of a background check with parents? You may want to say something like "Mr. Patel, I would love to have you volunteer any time. To protect all of the children in care, our state licensing agency requires that all of our volunteers submit to a criminal background check. Once you receive your clearance, please make a copy for me to place in my volunteer file."

Family Meetings

Another way to involve parents and guardians is to have a family meeting outside of your normal hours of operation. These meetings are generally held to allow families to get acquainted with each other and with you. Throughout the year, you can have family meetings with theme-based events or to organize a fundraiser or community event. Holiday parties, picnics, and family field trips are all wonderful ways to involve families. You may want to use these opportunities to do parenting workshops on topics such as play and child development or toilet learning.

Respect Cultures

Your willingness to allow parents to be their child's first teacher shows that you understand how important their roles are. You may not always understand or approve of a family's parenting style; however, you should always respect each family's diverse cultural views on parenting. Find out as much as you can about each child's culture and traditions. This information will help you be a more responsive caregiver. If a conflict happens because of a cultural difference, meet with the family to discuss a mutually agreeable solution for the issue.

Additionally, try to find ways to bring diversity into your child care setting. Try different foods, show children cultural photos, and incorporate arts-and-crafts activities and music from various cultures.

Reduce Conflict

There may be times when you and a parent disagree about a situation. Learning how to properly handle complaints or conflicts is critical. Not responding properly to a complaint or concern can be damaging to your business and will weaken the relationship between you and the family. It is important to take steps to reduce the likelihood of conflict.

- **Leave extra baggage at the door**. When you open for business, let go of anything that triggered a negative mood, such as an argument with a member of your family or negative news on the radio. Start each day with fresh, positive thoughts.

- **Pick your battles**. Inform parents of their child's challenging behaviors, but don't make the information negative each day. Parents like to hear positive messages about their child's day. Be selective about what information you send home about the child. Normal behavior that is challenging to you may not be information that needs to be reported. For example, parents are likely aware that their toddler says "no" quite often. Find ways to address these challenges without the parent's assistance. If the behavior persists and you have exhausted your resources, then ask the parents for suggestions. Document challenges and try to implement solutions so that parents can be informed about your attempt to resolve the issue.

- **Be open to constructive criticisms or concerns**. Parents may question why you implemented a policy or how you are caring for their child. They may also make suggestions or comments. Listen to them, and decide if their suggestions will benefit your program. Most parents chose you because of your professional ability; take their feedback as an opportunity for improvement. After evaluating any concerns, promptly respond to families about them.

- **Be proactive**. Attempt to work out differences before they escalate into a larger issue. If you are aware that a parent is feeling uneasy about the way you handled an issue, contact the parent to help resolve those feelings or explain why you made the decision.

- **Listen**. Show that you are listening by restating the questions. Wait until a parent asks for advice before offering it. Some parents are offended if you give unsolicited advice.

Things to Avoid

- Avoid taking sides in a divorce or separation.
- Avoid trying to win an argument or disagreement at all costs. The family may decide to terminate child care.
- Avoid showing favoritism among parents or children.
- Avoid never being available when parents are arriving or picking up the children.
- Avoid disrespecting the parents' views or cultural differences.
- Avoid disclosing personal information.
- Avoid confronting parents in a rude manner.

Handle Conflict

There is considerable trust in the child care business. Parents need to know that the lines of communication are open at all times. Parents who have concerns or complaints about you or someone in your program should receive prompt attention. Despite your best efforts to avoid it, conflict may occasionally arise. When it does, keep this action plan in mind.

1. Remain calm. Getting angry or losing your temper only makes things worse.

2. Maintain self-control.

3. Be respectful, even if the parents are not.

4. Reinforce the idea that you and the parents have the child's best interests in mind.

5. Act quickly to resolve the concern. If you can't discuss the concern immediately, set up a time to meet. Remember, other families should not be privy to a conflict that does not involve them.

6. Delay your meeting with a parent if you need to gather more information about the incident or complaint. Additionally, delaying your meeting gives time for both parties to calm down and evaluate the situation again before meeting.

7. Be willing to make a compromise unless it will jeopardize the welfare of the child or other children in your care.

Additional Resources

Two great books that can assist you with family relationship building are *Transition Magician for Families: Helping Parents and Children with Everyday Routines* by Ruth Chvojicek, Mary Henthorne, and Nola Larson (2001), and *Partnering with Parents: Easy Programs to Involve Parents in the Early Learning Process* by Bob Rockwell and Janet Rockwell Kniepkamp (2003).

11

Ensuring Safety

Providing a safe environment for the children in our care is critical. Children come to your facility ready to learn and explore. It is your responsibility to ensure that potential hazards are reduced and that you develop proactive safety strategies. You must think about the safety of the children, the parents, siblings, staff, and yourself. As a caregiver, it is your responsibility to have the proper safety guidelines in place to reduce hazards, injuries, and illnesses. In addition, children must be supervised at all times. Please check with your licensing agency regarding state-specific safety procedures.

In this section, I provide tips to reduce the likelihood of injury and illness. I recommend you create a safety checklist to ensure that everything is inspected and cleaned properly. These checklists can be used for daily, weekly, monthly, semiannual, and annual inspections. Here is an example list of items to be placed on your checklists:

Indoor Environment

Daily

☑ Open the windows to circulate fresh air.

☑ Vacuum the rugs and carpeting.

☑ Mop the floors.

☑ Clean the tables and high chairs.

☑ Check for damaged toys.

☑ Remove the trash.

☑ Check all safety latches and covers used each day.

☑ Wipe down the infant equipment.

Weekly

☑ Inspect for dust and wipe up any particles.

☑ Clean the cots or mats.

☑ Clean the kitchen appliances and throw away spoiled food.

☑ Clean and rotate the toys.

☑ Wash the blankets and pillow covers.

Monthly

☑ Inspect the floors, ceilings, and walls for moisture, mold, and mildew.

☑ Inspect the cribs, changing tables, and shelves for loose screws.

☑ Ensure that all latches on the cabinets are securely fastened.

☑ Inspect holes and dark spaces for rodents and insects.

☑ Vacuum your upholstered sofas and chairs to reduce dirt and grime.

☑ Clean rugs and carpeting as needed.

☑ Replace any first aid supplies.

Semiannually and Annually

☑ Inspect smoke detectors semiannually. (There should be at least one smoke detector located on each level of your home.)

☑ Inspect carpeting and rugs for loose threads or crumbled padding.

☑ Replace lightbulbs with ecofriendly ones.

☑ Clean curtains, valances, and window blinds.

☑ Inspect the carbon monoxide detector.

Ongoing

☑ Keep a first aid kit in an easily accessible location.

☑ Quickly clean any spills with the proper cleaning supplies.

☑ Ensure that storage cabinets are tightly secured to the wall.

☑ Label everything in your environment, especially items in the storage cabinet.

☑ Ensure that cleaning supplies and other potential hazards are secured in a locked cabinet.

☑ Replace worn or damaged toys and equipment.

☑ Make any repairs to play areas and workstations as soon as possible.

☑ Whenever you renovate or make a repair to an area, be sure to check for small particles or sharp edges that could have been overlooked by your repair technician.

☑ Provide a detailed cleaning plan for the kitchen and restrooms.

☑ Have a list of emergency service phone numbers readily available.

Outdoor Environment

☑ Follow the same child-to-caregiver ratios as you use for indoor play.

☑ Keep all children within a caregiver's sight at all times.

☑ Position a caregiver nearby if the children are using a slide or other playground apparatus.

☑ Have additional caregivers when the children are using a pool or participating in a water activity. (Ask for a parent volunteer for these types of activities.)

☑ Keep a first aid kit outdoors.

☑ Ensure that each child riding a tricycle or bike is wearing a helmet.

☑ Inspect sandboxes and water tables for bugs and pet waste. Keep sandboxes covered and water tables drained when not in use.

☑ Clean the sandbox and pet areas.

☑ Clean the play yard.

☑ Use only natural fertilizers and insecticides when treating your lawn and plants.

☑ Check your play yard prior to use for downed power lines, stray animals, and trash.

Additional Safety Tips

Each year children are hurt because of unsafe indoor and outdoor environments. Here are several tips to add to your safety checklist:

• Maintain proper staff ratios. Proper supervision of children is important because caregivers will be able to monitor the children, prevent accidents, and reduce injuries before they happen.

- Never leave children unattended.

- Ensure that your home is lead and asbestos free.

- Use the proper techniques for handling food and snacks, such as proper hand washing, wearing gloves, labeling food, and preventing cross-contamination by keeping meats and other foods separate.

- Clean and sanitize areas where mold and bacteria can build up and pose a hazard.

- Use electrical outlets properly. Use outlet covers when outlets are not in use.

- Test the water temperature at the sinks the children will use. Water heaters should be set to a maximum of 120 degrees Fahrenheit.

- Childproof play spaces by crawling around the entire area on your knees to detect hazards.

- Properly store firearms in the home in a locked area well away from the child care space. Ammunition should be kept locked in a separate area.

- Replace broken pacifiers and bottle nipples. Young children often chew these nipples, which could cause a safety hazard.

- Use safety gates, partitions, or furniture to block children's access to potentially harmful areas, such as the kitchen or a stairway.

- Look for lingering food in toddlers' mouths after lunches and snacks. Children sometimes hold food in their mouths long after they eat. It's important to do a visual check after a meal to prevent choking.

- Arrange the environment to prevent running. Use partitions, tables, or shelving to reduce running in your physical space. Be sure to have an area available for large-motor activities.

- Keep several ice packs in the freezer. You never know when you may have to use them for minor accidents.

Adult Safety Tips

If an adult falls on your property, it can lead to major injuries and potential lawsuits. Please check walkways and entrances daily. Be sure to check stairways for any loose nails or obstructions. Install handrails and check existing handrails and stairways for areas that need repairs. Keep your walkways well lit and free of snow, water, or debris that could make them hazardous.

One of the moms at my child care home was walking down the stairs to pick up her child when the heel of her shoe caught on a nail from the stair edge and she tumbled down the steps. Thank goodness she was okay. Another child care provider's customer walked down the steps and tripped on the safety gate's frame and broke her ankle. The safety gate was attached to the bottom steps as a deterrent for the children but wound up being an obstacle for a parent.

You can't predict when an accident may occur. Keep your eyes and ears open for potential dangers that may be present. In these situations, it is imperative to have the proper liability and homeowners insurance.

Reduce Your Risks

You are exposed to viruses, body fluids, and hazardous conditions throughout the day. To reduce your risk of illness and injury, consider receiving training on the proper techniques for

- lifting children and heavy items;
- storing hazardous items;
- cleaning up spills and bodily fluids;
- reporting illnesses;
- using documentation to report an accident;
- using proper diapering techniques;
- using proper toileting techniques;
- maintaining safe sleeping arrangements for infants and toddlers.

In addition to these items, ensure you have an adult-size chair available for use throughout the day. Spending most of your time on the floor and kneeling to the children's eye level can strain your back.

Pet Safety

Pets are a great addition to a family child care program. There are many providers who have family pets and share those pets with the children in their care. Please check with your local licensing department regarding any pets that may be banned from child care homes.

- Notify parents of any pets you have in your home and inform them any time you decide to bring a pet into your home.
- Maintain and record your pets' vaccinations.
- Supervise children around pets at all times.
- Remind children to wash their hands after handling pets.
- Keep aggressive pets away from children. You may have to purchase a kennel or cage.

- Keep sick animals away from children.

- Place pets away from the children during meals and snacktimes.

- Keep litter boxes, pet food, and large cages away from the children.

- Maintain your pets' space to reduce odor and waste in your family child care.

Create a Plan for Emergency Procedures

In the event of an emergency, it is a good to a have plan of action. Each plan will be unique to your family child care and the types of emergency conditions that could occur in your area. Please follow your child care licensing manual for proper emergency procedures in your state.

- Prepare a blueprint or diagram of your home. Clearly label the windows and doors that will serve as emergency exits.

- Make a list of emergency contact people to call for assistance if you are alone in your child care program.

- Set up an evacuation plan.

- Determine a destination outside of your home where everyone will meet.

- Make a copy of each child's information card and photo. Place them in a waterproof bag to carry with you.

- Practice emergency evacuations, fire drills, and tornado drills once per month. Log this information.

- Create an emergency preparedness kit, including water, nonperishable food, a can opener, a radio with batteries, a first aid kit, small toys, books, infant formula, bottles, and blankets.

*Tip | Maintaining a safe environment is the best approach to reducing accidents and injuries. Ensure that the children in your care and your own family are practicing safety daily. Stay proactive and be alert to unexpected changes. Remain calm and implement your plan of action. Remember, safety is our first priority when working with young children.

12

Creating Learning Environments

Now that you have taken steps to plan for your child care business and reviewed the important safety tips, let's look at creating indoor and outdoor environments that will support the development of the children in your care. How will you arrange your equipment and materials? Where will the children participate in activities? The organization of your learning environments says a lot about the quality of your program. They are a direct reflection of your style and early childhood practices. Design your spaces with safety in mind. You must be able to properly supervise all of the children in your care at all times. Remember, well-planned learning environments not only foster learning, but also reduce discipline problems.

There are many things to consider when you create an environment, including the following:

- the ages of the children

- storage of supplies

- storage of toys and equipment

- meal preparation areas

- lighting

- colors

Areas should be flexible, safe, and comfortable while offering children many learning choices. Before beginning, review your state licensing standards regarding safety and space requirements. Also, contact your licensing consultant prior to beginning a new renovation or major change to your current licensed family child care. If you have children with special needs in your program, you may decide to make small modifications to your home. Please see the ADA (www.ada.gov) for more information. The following are general tips to keep in mind as you design learning environments:

- Leave room for flexibility. Keeping your environment flexible will allow you to change your room arrangements for different activities. Use furniture as dividers if necessary.

- Place eating and food preparation areas away from the restroom or diaper-changing areas. If possible, place diaper-changing stations near the restroom or a sink.

- Label your storage systems and lock anything that could be a potential hazard to children. Storage for additional supplies and equipment is essential to your environment.

- Decide on carpeting or hard-surface flooring. It's best to place tile or hard flooring in the restrooms, eating areas, and craft areas. Carpeting, rugs, or foam-filled mats can be used in the infant/toddler spaces or anywhere children will be playing on the floor.

- Label everything in the environment. Children will learn how to keep things organized and the print will add to their language and literacy skills. A great idea is to use combination picture and word labels. If the children are learning a second language, or if you have children whose first language is not English, it's a great idea make labels in those languages as well.

- Post pictures of the children in a variety of locations to support self-esteem and allow them to reflect on prior learning experiences. When posting pictures, include a brief narrative or summary of the interactions or experiences.

- Make sure that you post children's artwork or decor at their eye level. Try to avoid having too many items on the wall. This can be overstimulating and look cluttered.

- Decorate your room with seasonal art or themes. Ask the children to assist you.

- Select materials and purchase items that are unique. You can purchase items from early childhood supply catalogs and outlets.

- Provide open-ended materials that allow children unlimited possibilities and outcomes. Examples include manipulatives or table toys, blocks, art materials, recycled items, sand, water, and other natural elements. Be very selective when purchasing battery-operated toys. These types of toys limit children's play with closed-ended results.

- Select materials that are durable and safe.

- Make sure all infant and toddler equipment is washable.

- Rotate toys monthly or bimonthly to refresh your environment. But don't change favorites out of the environment. They will surely be missed.

- Use your ceilings to hang mobiles. This is a great area to decorate.

- Purchase a washable sofa cover to reduce germs and wear and tear if you use your sofa during child care.

Multipurpose Areas

By their nature, family child care programs are multipurpose because you're using part of your home for the care of the children. One challenge lies in trying to balance home spaces and child care spaces. Ask your own family for suggestions about which areas they are willing to devote to child care and which areas they prefer to keep for family use only. Family members should help you maintain the rooms that serve as both family and child care spaces.

One problem with multipurpose space is trying to eliminate overcrowding and clutter. You probably know that children can quickly become overstimulated if there are too many things in one area. Family child care providers have to use lots of creativity when setting up their environments. Your kitchen area may serve as the eating area and also the art area. You may want to purchase a storage unit on wheels that can be used to store the children's plates, cups, and bowls or their arts-and-crafts materials. Your living room can double as a rest area for the children. A coat closet can be used to store the children's blankets or mats. Purchase a small shed for storing outdoor child care equipment. Keeping your supplies and equipment organized will reduce clutter and make your child care space a safe and fun environment. Now let's turn our attention to specific areas of your home.

Outdoor Entrance

As parents and children approach your house, they should be impressed by the warm, aesthetically pleasing quality of your front entrance. Beautiful flowers and shrubs, a fresh cut lawn, and such details as a welcome mat, wreath, chimes, child-centered decorations, or small decorative flags give a sneak peak of what's to come. Periodically, check the pathways and lawn for anything that may give a negative impression of your home, such as weeds, trash, or cracks in the walkways. Clean and clutter-free areas increase the safety and aesthetics of your child care home.

Indoor Entrance

A foyer or entrance provides a transition from the outside to the inside and should be welcoming and comforting. As families enter your home, there should be something in the entrance that attracts both children and adults. You may want to have a nice flower arrangement, child-friendly decorations, and pictures of your family or the child care families. Depending on the size of your space, you may also want to add a small table or use wall space to create a parent board that displays newsletters, menus, or parent notes. Just be sure to keep it organized and clutter free. This is also a great area to showcase an aquarium or other natural elements. If you have a closet or wall, place small hooks for the children to store their outdoor clothing.

Set the Mood

There are many ways to create wonderful learning experiences for children. A great start is to determine how you will use significant components in an indoor environment, such as lighting, color, and sound.

- Light is important in child care settings. Children need both natural and artificial light throughout the day. Take advantage of sunny days by allowing sunshine to filter into your rooms. This brightness can bring joy and stimulation to children. Change your incandescent bulbs to ecofriendly, compact fluorescent bulbs to save energy and promote a healthy environment. During naptime, try using natural light, a low-wattage lamp, or nightlight for a calm, serene setting.

- Color is powerful because it can help set the mood. Take the time to review color choices that will work best with your child care home. A good rule of thumb is to use pastel or light color choices, such as blues, whites, yellows, pink, grays, and tans, on the walls and ceilings and add colorful accents with materials and equipment. You can also use color to define spaces and separate learning centers. Try not to be color biased by using only your favorite color throughout the setting.

- Children engaged in active play will bring all types of sounds into your environment. As caregivers, we know too well how sound can affect a child's disposition. While children should be seen and heard, too much noise can lead to behavior problems. It is important to find a balance. Aim to group noisy areas together. For example, you might group the music and the block areas in the same general area. You'll also want to ensure that children have quiet and peaceful moments throughout the day. Your napping and reading areas should be placed away from noisy activities.

Children's Play Areas

Many family child care homes offer care to multiple ages of children. This creates a challenge when trying to ensure that you are meeting the needs of each child in your care. Each age group should have developmentally appropriate areas in which to play and developmentally appropriate materials to explore. It's okay to use a large room for all of the children in your care as long as you set aside time and space to offer children age-appropriate activities and materials, such as naps, block play, and art activities, while making sure the room is safe and comfortable for all of the children. Use developmental milestones to help determine each child's needs. Depending on the size and space limitations of your home, you may have to rearrange special fixtures or furniture to accommodate children. Proper storage and child-friendly accessories help maintain a safe atmosphere and an organized playroom.

There are family child care providers who have large areas, such as their lower level or basement, to use to separate infants, toddlers, preschoolers, and school-age children. The key to separation is great supervision and developmentally appropriate toys and equipment in each area.

Infant Area

An infant area should be spacious enough to accommodate cribs and still allow ample space for floor activities. Bright colors, various textures, and soft materials work well to stimulate infant learning. Purchase items that are durable and washable. Soft lighting and natural lighting work best in this area. An infant area should be placed in a quiet section of your child care home. You might want to have a small storage area for infant supplies and equipment. Be sure to place objects that could pose a threat or choking hazard away from infant play spaces. For more information, see chapter 11. Here are key materials to support an infant area:

- cribs

- changing tables

- bouncing seats

- storage bins for diapers and clothing

- age-appropriate toys, such as blocks, rattles, balls, dolls, mirrored toys, and squeeze toys

- high chairs

- mats or blankets for floor activities

- mobiles

- textured toys

- stimulating music

- picture books

- teething rings

- cloth puppets

Toddler Area

A toddler area should be designed for active toddler play. The physical space for toddlers should be inviting and secure with boundaries that help support play, exploration, creativity, and rest. A toddler's curiosity should be supported with an open space to allow for mobility while she explores increasing independence. Offer small nooks and quiet areas for toddlers to "hang out." You will also need duplicate toys and equipment to minimize conflict. Toddlers enjoy place spaces that allow them to imitate adults and animals and experience the world in which they live. Toddlers are very curious about their environments, and a good rule of thumb regarding toys and equipment for this age is if the toy can fit inside of a tissue roll, then it is unsafe for infants and toddlers. For more safety tips, please see chapter 11. The following are key materials to support a toddler area:

- blocks

- trucks

- small tables with child-size chairs

- unbreakable mirrors

- push/pull toys, textured toys, and stacking toys

- knob puzzles

- dolls

- dress-up clothes, including hats and shoes

- books

- interactive music

- large beads with string

- large manipulatives and building materials

- shape sorters

- peg boards

- age-appropriate art supplies, such as crayons, finger paints, and markers

- dramatic play props, such as telephones, dishes, and transportation vehicles

Preschooler Area

Like toddlers, preschoolers need vigorous movement. They need areas to freely explore the world around them and challenges that will enable them to develop their physical and mental abilities. Preschoolers also need large open spaces and small nooks for special times. They also need many opportunities to support their growing independence and social-emotional development. Preschoolers have the ability to explore many different types of materials and equipment. Be sure to determine that all items are safe, nontoxic, and developmentally appropriate. Here are key materials to support a preschooler area:

- manipulatives, such as Lego pieces, beading materials, and linking loops

- blocks

- writing tools

- art supplies, such as paint, crayons, and collage materials

- science items, such as scales, magnifying glasses, and nonfiction books

- sensory materials, such as playdough, sand, and water

- reading and language materials, such as picture books, children's dictionaries, and books on tape or CD

- dolls

- dramatic play props, including kitchen materials, dress-up clothes, purses and bags, and play money

- child-size tables and chairs

- quiet-area items, such as big pillows, puzzles, and books

- mats for rough and tumble play

- toys, including small plastic or wooden animals, people, and houses

- musical instruments

Print-Rich Environment

A print-rich environment offers children the opportunity to see print in every area of the child care home. You can have the children assist you with labeling areas that are used as your child care space. These words will become more familiar to them as they see them in their environment. You can label all of the children's shelves, sinks, coatracks, toy containers, and storage containers. If you have a multilingual environment, you may want to label the areas in a different language.

Learning Centers

On the following pages I describe seven main learning centers. There are additional learning centers that are used separately or in combination with the main learning centers. Incorporate other centers as space, time, or finances permit. As you set up learning centers, keep the ages and developmental stages of the children in mind. Not all of the materials are suitable for all children. You would obviously not allow toddlers to play with small beads in a manipulative center.

Dramatic Play

The dramatic play center allows children to imitate and exchange roles. They learn to act out different scenarios about the world in which they live. This type of play helps children develop self-esteem, self-confidence, and social-emotional skills, and it also supports cognitive development. The following is a list of suggested items for a dramatic play area:

- dress-up clothing
- hats
- shoes
- mirrors
- aprons
- dolls
- puppets
- kitchen sets
- cleaning tools, such as a mop and broom
- telephones
- toy food items and empty, clean food containers
- books
- pictures

- writing tools

- notebooks

- play menus

- maps

- old junk mail

- pots and pans

- costume jewelry

- paper shopping bags

- music

Block Play

The block play center incorporates many variations of blocks and toys. This area is closely related to the dramatic play center because of the way children use blocks and toys to imitate and construct things they see in their world. Block play builds on children's exploration abilities, problem-solving skills, large- and small-motor development, and language. The following is a list of suggested items for the block area:

- blocks of all sizes, shapes, colors, and textures

- items for building bridges, ponds, and highways, such as cardboard, fabric, and construction paper
- cars, trucks, and boats
- traffic signs
- toy people
- toy animals

Music Play

The music center should be used any time during daily activities. This center involves dancing, clapping, singing, stomping, and any type of creative expression. Children learn language development, physical development, social-emotional skills, and creativity through music and movement. There are many types of music offerings for children from children's classical to rock to rhythm and blues. I have also found that children enjoy listening to music from different parts of the world. The following is a list of suggested items for a music center:

- musical recordings
- rattles
- tambourines
- drums
- keyboards
- handmade musical instruments
- rhythm sticks
- boxes
- scarves
- streamers
- headphones
- a tape recorder
- a CD player

Language and Literacy Play

This area is a must-have for young learners. Children really enjoy a great story. Literacy activities allow children to learn language, small- and large-motor development, creative expression, critical thinking skills, and social-emotional development. The language and literacy center can include the following items:

- books of all types, especially picture books

- writing tools

- paper

- a flannelboard

- puppets

- soft pillows or bean bags

- a rug

- a tape recorder or CD player and headphones

- books on tape or CD

Manipulative Play

The manipulative center is a wonderful place to explore mathematical concepts and problem-solving skills. The children use hand-eye coordination to build, connect, count, and group small pieces to promote meaningful learning. The following is a list of suggested items for a manipulative center:

- puzzles

- games

- Lego pieces

- gears

- dominoes

- small bowls

- measuring cups

- scales

- spoons

- pegs and pegboards

- colored beads

- magnets

Creative Art Play

An art center allows children the opportunity to experiment with many objects and art supplies. Children learn best through open-ended art activities. These types of activities allow children to use their creative expression and representation of objects in their world. Simply provide materials and allow children to make their own creations. The following is a list of suggested items for an art center:

- paint
- clay
- string
- paper
- crayons
- brushes
- age-appropriate scissors
- Velcro
- glue
- tape
- wrapping paper
- boxes
- clean egg cartons
- ribbon
- cardboard
- beads
- fabric
- easels
- sponges

Science Play

The science center in a family child care program can really be a haven of exploration. Children of all ages can learn from materials and equipment that support science. You may want to add real animals, such as fish, hermit crabs, or butterfly exhibits. You may also want to give families an opportunity to stock the science center with items from their homes or items found while exploring with their young ones. Items in your science center can be very broad. Here is a list of some items for a science center:

- magnifying glasses
- test tubes
- tweezers
- netting

- small plastic jars with lids

- food coloring

- chalk

- a variety of boxes

- assorted magnets

- markers

- graphing paper

- tape

- paper

- crayons

- feathers

- insects

- soil

- rocks

- clay

Outdoor Learning Environments

The outdoor environment can be an extension of your indoor environment. It should have the same welcoming feel as your indoor spaces. Natural elements stimulate learning and curiosity. Incorporate a garden, flower beds, or places to dig and pour. Special touches, such as a whimsical scarecrow, make the play area inviting for children.

Don't be afraid to bring some of your indoor activities outside. You should also offer a variety of age-appropriate equipment. However, as with indoor spaces, be careful not to overcrowd your outdoor play space with too much equipment. Children need lots of room for active play, such as running, crawling, and free exploration.

Outdoor play areas should be designed for safety and comfort. Be sure to inspect your outdoor environment before allowing the children to play in it. There have been instances when I have had to change our schedule due to a telephone repair person in the yard or fallen baby birds. You will also want to look for downed power lines, large tree branches, or other potentially dangerous objects that could harm young children. For more safety tips, see chapter 11. Ensure that kennels are locked and cleaned daily and pools and ponds are out of the children's reach. A covered trash bin and a handy caddy are excellent additions to your outdoor environment. The caddy is useful for toting wipes, tissues, hand sanitizer, child information cards, a pen, small notebook, cordless phone, camera, and first aid kit. Here is a list of equipment to stimulate outdoor learning:

- climbers
- slides
- swings
- riding equipment with helmets
- balls
- cars
- art supplies
- sand and water tables (keep sand tables covered when not in use and drain water daily)
- parachutes
- bug catchers (assist children with the capture and release of insects and instruct them on observation only)
- mats
- push-pull toys
- jump ropes
- tunnels
- child-size tables and chairs

Whatever else you do, don't hesitate to personalize your child care space. Items such as quilts and art or a whimsical garden decoration make children's play spaces more comfortable and inviting. It also demonstrates your passion for young children. Invite the children to help make things around the home to support their development.

Additional Resources

There are child care design books you can refer to. One valuable resource is *Designs for Living and Learning: Transforming Early Childhood Environments* by Deb Curtis and Margie Carter (2003).

I also recommend visiting a variety of child care settings to get ideas and observe how different areas function together to support quality care. Many colleges, universities, and churches offer on-site, quality child care and would allow you to visit their facilities.

13

Planning Daily Activities

A common question among new family child care providers is "What will I do with the children all day?" Planning fun and exciting activities for children will become easier as your experience grows. And you will find that young children enjoy repetition.

Daily Schedules

Daily schedules should be used only as an outline for the day. One of the best ways to support children's learning is to listen to and follow their cues. Allow children the opportunity to explore their environment by offering child-directed programing. There will be times when children do not want to stop playing with the building blocks or puzzles to move to another activity. A flexible schedule will allow for these times. You may want to allow small groups or individual children to play in various centers rather than having all of the children engage in the same activity at the same time. The key is to allow children the opportunity to direct their own learning, which is more meaningful to them than adult-directed learning.

Infants and Toddlers

While your schedule should be flexible, there are daily routines that must be performed throughout the day. These include eating, diapering/toilet use, napping, and hand washing. You may want to build your schedule around these daily routines. Take a look at the sample schedule for infants and toddlers that follows. Their schedules are less structured than those of older children and offer more opportunities for napping and routines such as feeding and toileting. Diapering is one of the daily routines in a child care schedule and an activity where children bond, build trust, and develop social interactions with a responsive caregiver. Diapering and toileting should be included in the schedule as needed or at least every two hours. Responsive caregiving will build the confidence children need to properly learn toileting practices.

Sample Daily Schedule for Infants and Toddlers

7:30–8:30	Arrival and greeting time Feeding time or tummy time (infants)
Exploration time	Play on blankets (infants) Play with age-appropriate toys and equipment (toddlers)
Breakfast	Bathroom break and hand washing Bottle feeding (infants) or breakfast (toddlers)
Exploration time	Play with age-appropriate toys (infants) Play with toys or musical instruments (toddlers)
Outdoor play	Rest on blankets, take a stroll in the yard, or swing in an infant swing (infants) Play with toys, such as large trucks and push toys, or on climbers and slides (toddlers)
Lunchtime	Bathroom break and hand washing Bottle feeding (infants) or lunch (toddlers)
Nap	Listen to stories or get a massage (infants and toddlers)
Group time	Listen to stories, recite fingerplays, or play games such as peekaboo (infants and toddlers)
Snacktime	Bathroom break and hand washing Bottle feeding (infants) or snack (toddlers)
Outdoor play or Exploration time	Age-appropriate art activities or water play (infants and toddlers)
Departure time	Greet parents Report on the daily schedule

Preschoolers

Preschoolers also need child-directed activities. They enjoy consistency, structure in their activities, and flexible schedules. The following schedule is outlined for preschool children. Preschool schedules should allow for more independent self-help skills and spontaneous play.

Sample Daily Schedule for Preschoolers

7:00–9:00	Arrival, breakfast, and exploration time (children choose activities)
9:00–10:00	Large-group activities, such as circle time, reading, and fingerplays
10:00–10:30	Hand washing, morning snack, and clean up
10:30–11:30	Outdoor play, games, art activities, reading, science, large- and small-group play
11:30–12:30	Hand washing and lunch
12:30–1:00	Story time
1:00–3:00	Nap
3:00–3:30	Hand washing and snack
3:30–4:30	Exploration time or outdoor play
4:30–6:00	Exploration time and departures

Learning Centers

In addition to a daily plan of activities, you may also have learning centers set up where children can explore and play by themselves or with other children. In a family child care environment, these learning centers may overlap due to space limitations. Just be sure to place noisy centers, such as music and blocks, together and quiet centers, such as language and manipulatives, together. You may also have equipment for your learning centers stored in a box that can be set up daily when the children arrive. For more information about where to place supplies and equipment for each age group, please see chapter 12.

Activities for Mixed-Age Groups

Offering activities for mixed-age groups can sometimes be challenging. There are many activities you can do together such as music and movement, fingerplays, and water play. You can also read stories and take walks. Other activities may need modifications to increase or decrease the level of mastery. For a game of catch, you may need to use a larger and softer ball for toddlers than you would for a preschool child. Toddlers may enjoy this game better if the ball is rolled to them.

Cooking is another activity to get everyone involved in. The preschool children may help with counting and measuring while the toddlers may pour and mix. Your infants can participate by playing with the textures, grasping the spoons and measuring cups, or by observing the activity.

Theme-Based Activities

A theme can be created for one day, one week, or even the entire month. Theme-based activities are great when planning for a field trip. For example, you may have a field trip planned for a farm. Your theme for the month can be Barnyard Fun. Children can decorate their learning environments with farm-related art. You can incorporate the farm theme into your learning centers by adding toys and equipment to support the theme. For example, add books about farming and farm animals to the literacy center. Place toy farm animals and tractors in the block area. Farm costumes, animal puppets, and children's gardening tools can be added to the dramatic play center.

Handmade Materials

Handmade materials are a great addition to any family child care program. These materials bring less commercialization to a home program. Making handmade materials and toys also shows families your passion for children's learning. There are many items that can be easily handmade. Here is a list of the more common ones:

- musical instruments
- microphones
- fingerplay puppets
- quilts and blankets
- dramatic play costumes
- matching games
- signs and bulletin board materials
- decorations

Be sure to take advantage of teachable moments. Teachable moments are those spontaneous events that we didn't plan for in a day. For example, a neighbor is having a new driveway poured with concrete. This is an excellent time to take the children near the site to see the large trucks and to learn about the science behind concrete.

14

Buying Groceries and Planning Meals

As a family child care provider, one of your goals is to offer children nutritious meals and snacks. There may be providers who do not serve meals to children, but most of us are responsible for ensuring a quality meal plan for the children in our care. Meal planning takes time and practice. There are many things to consider when planning meals, such as nutrition guidelines and serving sizes for children, menus, convenience, cost, and food handling and storage.

Understand Nutritional Guidelines for Children

When planning meals, you need to determine what foods will give children the nutrients needed for proper growth and development. According to the family child care component of the federal Child and Adult Care Food Program, there are four main food categories: milk, fruits/vegetables, grains/breads, and meat/meat alternatives. Meat alternatives include proteins, such as nuts, beans, and dairy products. These food categories will offer children a large variety of foods and allow you to create great meal combinations. The following page lists sample items that can be served in each category.

Foods from the Four Main Food Groups

Milk	Fruits/Vegetables	Grains/Breads	Meat/Meat Alternatives
whole milk	pears	muffins	cooked beans
2% milk	apples or applesauce	French toast	cheese or cottage cheese
1% milk	peaches	wheat or white bread	beef
skim milk	plums or prunes	pizza crust	chicken
cultured buttermilk	apricots	pancakes or waffles	pork
	Brussels sprouts	oatmeal or grits	turkey
	spinach	crackers	fish
	broccoli	bagels	eggs
	green beans	pasta	nuts
	carrots	biscuits	yogurt

Know Serving Sizes

Many children in our nation are obese in part because they have been given larger servings than those recommended by the U.S. Department of Agriculture. The size of a serving depends on the food category and the child's age. A serving size for a two-year-old at breakfast is

- one-half cup of milk
- one-quarter cup of fruit or vegetables
- one-quarter cup of cereal

It is important to follow the proper serving sizes for the children in your care. Overfeeding or underfeeding children can lead to poor nutrition and the risk of illness or eating disorders. For more information about serving size, visit www.MyPyramid.gov.

Establish Menus

When planning menus, aim to combine food from different groups for each meal.

For example, serve chicken and broccoli casserole, fruit milk shakes, beef stew, or vegetable soup with noodles. These combinations are easy to prepare and meet the nutritional meal requirements from the Child and Adult Care Food Program (CACFP). The CACFP offers home- and center-based providers the opportunity to receive food reimbursements for preparing meals for children. The amount of the reimbursement varies depending on the number of children in your care and the income levels of the families enrolled in your program. This is an excellent way to reduce your food expenses. CACFP requires that you serve nutritious meals and snacks that are appropriate for the ages of the children in your program. CACFP requests that you take attendance at point of service and maintain a daily menu. A local agency of the CACFP will make visits to your home to determine compliance and provide you with resources and nutritional news to support your meal planning. Please check with your local Food Program office or visit www.cacfp.org to determine eligibility.

Sample Five-Day Menu

Day of the Week	Breakfast	Lunch	Snack
Monday	oranges pancakes milk	spaghetti with ground turkey carrot sticks broccoli milk	cheese crackers juice
Tuesday	apple slices oatmeal milk	baked chicken peas egg noodles peaches milk	bread sticks milk
Wednesday	banana toast milk	macaroni and cheese spinach applesauce milk	fruit cocktail wheat crackers
Thursday	strawberries muffins milk	tortilla beef and cheese lettuce and tomatoes nectarines milk	animal crackers carrot and celery sticks
Friday	watermelon biscuits milk	veggie egg rolls rice cheese sticks milk	plum slices milk

You and the families of the children in your care can determine the meals you serve. It's a great idea to ask parents for a list of their child's favorite foods when planning meals. Some children are picky eaters, so gradually add new foods to the menu for the children to try. Another great way to get your finicky eaters to try something different is to have the children help you prepare meals. When I first began caring for children, I would set aside Thursdays as our cooking day. We would make creative meals and snacks on this day. There are a variety of cookbooks for children on the market today. In addition, be sure to offer culturally rich foods. Page 98 shows a simple five-day menu for a preschool child. Visit www.MyPyramid .gov for more children's meal ideas.

Plan for Convenience

Most providers are looking for ways to reduce their time in the kitchen. Here are a few time-saving options when planning meals:

- Make a list of all the menu items needed for the month and buy nonperishable foods in one shopping trip.
- Complete the prep work for several meals at one time.
- Purchase an additional freezer to store food then double or triple recipes and freeze meals to serve later.
- Purchase items according to the amount of servings that each item yields.
- Rotate meals that are popular with the children throughout the year.
- Plan meals that take less than thirty minutes to prepare.
- Plan meals that can be baked.

Stay Aware of Costs

Meals are a large expense for family child care providers. We are always looking for ways to cut costs while maintaining healthy menus. All states offer the CACFP to help supplement the cost of serving food to children in child care facilities. The food reimbursement allows providers to make sound nutritional choices when shopping for food. Use these tips to stretch your food dollars:

- Prepare an estimated budget for each meal and shop around for the highest quality of food at the lowest price.
- Make homemade food, such as bread, applesauce, and soup. These are items that children can help prepare.
- Try shopping at bulk food warehouses. I found the best quality for the lowest price at bulk food warehouses and local fresh food markets.

- Carry a shopping list and stick to it. Try to resist impulse buys.

- Reduce shopping expenses by preparing meals with similar ingredients.

- Clip coupons to reduce your grocery bill. Shop at stores that double coupons for your favorite items, and visit Web sites that offer downloadable coupons.

- Purchase smaller amounts of perishable foods to reduce spoilage.

- Reduce your shopping to once per week to avoid impulse purchases.

Food Storage

Proper food storage is essential to the health and safety of children. Be sure to read the labels to determine the shelf life and proper storage of food and beverages. Look for extra storage space in areas of your kitchen or pantry. Depending on the number of children in your care, you may need additional space to store food for your family child care program. As your business grows, you may need to purchase an additional freezer to place bulk items and large purchases to reduce costs and save time. When storing food items, be sure to label each item with the date of purchase.

Safety Tips for Food Handling

- Wash hands before and after cooking and serving food to children.

- Keep food areas clean, paying special attention to cracks and jointed areas where food particles can become trapped.

- Wipe all food areas with a disinfectant cleaning solution after use.

- Use the clean, rinse, and sanitize method when washing dishes.

- Air dry dishes and utensils after washing to reduce germs, or use your dishwasher's dry cycle.

- Throw away food that is past its "use by" date.

- Keep foods above 140 degrees Fahrenheit for cooking and serving, and reduce the temperature to under 40 degrees Fahrenheit for refrigeration.

- Place cooked foods in the refrigerator after two hours.

- Discard any leftover foods that were served to children.

- Do not place baby bottles in the microwave. Use a warmer or hot water to heat the bottle.

- Label all baby food and bottles with the child's name and date.

Be Aware of Food Allergies

Food allergies have increased over the years. Please be sure to ask families about any potential food allergies that could cause a reaction for their children. Sometimes food allergies are so severe that we need to alter our menus to accommodate the children. This is especially true with peanut and wheat allergies. Create a list of children who have food allergies and post the list in the kitchen and food-service areas. Ensure that you meet with the families to determine the best plan of action in the event their child has an allergic reaction.

15

Planning Field Trips

Field trips allow children to explore the world in which they live. Family child care providers who participate in field trips can offer children the hands-on experience of meaningful learning outside of the child care setting. There are many places to take young children. The most common are zoos, children's museums, farms, children's concerts, and community festivals. Check your local newspapers and parent magazines for great places to take children. I also found terrific ideas at the local library. Here are several helpful tips to make your field trip experiences enjoyable.

Do Your Research

The first important tip is to research the field trip prior to arrival. Take a drive to the location to determine if traffic, construction, or detours will delay your trip. Visit the area and look for restroom facilities, accommodations for children with special needs, and potential safety hazards. Also determine if there is adequate space for a group lunch.

Prepare for the Trip

Call your destination two days before to confirm the itinerary and check for cancellations or any unexpected changes to the schedule. You may want to prepare a small emergency kit, which includes a cell phone, child information cards, wipes, extra clothing, tissues, a small amount of first aid supplies, and hand sanitizer. Determine how you are going to transport the children. A reputable bus company is best. If you decide to allow parents to drive the children on the field trip, there are a few things you want to check before you designate parent drivers:

- Be sure that all the parents have been notified that their children will be driven by car pool or parent chaperones.

- The parents you designate to drive should have car insurance, a driver's license, and a good safety record. Ultimately, you are responsible for each child who attends a field trip. You want to ensure they are in good hands.

- If a parent doesn't pass the necessary clearances, invite them to meet you at the field trip location, or they can ride along with you or another parent.

Get Parents' Permission

A permission slip is needed to document that a parent has given you consent to take a child from the child care premises to another location. It is imperative that you have a signed permission slip for each child who attends. A permission slip should include the following information:

1. The date of the field trip
2. The location of the field trip
3. The cost of the field trip
4. The type of transportation
5. The due date for the permission slip
6. A parent's signature

Recruit Chaperones

Parents and guardians should be encouraged to attend the field trip. Give the permission slip to the parents at least two weeks in advance, just in case parents would like to request time off work to attend. A one-to-three or one-to-four chaperone-child ratio is ideal for children of all ages on a field trip. This gives the children more opportunities to explore, and it will give you peace of mind regarding supervision. Chaperones should be grouped with children who will be a good fit when paired along with their own child. You and your assistants should probably handle the children who are more rambunctious and energetic and need extra supervision. Make sure the chaperones are comfortable with the number and personalities of the children in their care. Parents or guardians who are going to be chaperones should complete a criminal background check. You can refer them to your local police department or human services agency for clearance.

Maintain Supervision

As a precaution, maintain an accurate attendance sheet that includes all of the children and chaperones in attendance. Make a note of any changes that occur, such as switching a child to a different chaperone or a child leaving with a parent or guardian. Most often, children get lost or are left at facilities because of inaccurate head counts or an adult assuming a child is with another adult. Teach the parents or guardians how to count the children periodically and ask them to stay with you in a large group whenever possible. Remember, they are chaperones, but you are responsible for the children.

A good rule of thumb is to perform a child count at these times:

- before you leave your facility

- on the bus ride to the location

- at the location

- during restroom breaks

- before you leave the field trip

- once you return to your child care facility

*Tip | If you decide to take your children to a place where there will be large groups present, it is a good idea to purchase brightly colored T-shirts with your facility's name and phone number.

If possible, take strollers and wagons to carry small children, diaper bags, lunches, and blankets.

Bring extra money for miscellaneous expenses.

Don't forget your camera! You can take photos of the children enjoying the event and make them into an album for the language and literacy center, post them on a bulletin board, or use them in your newsletter.

Field trips can be a lot of work. Proper planning and safe guidelines help ensure a fantastic trip. It also will be a wonderful memory for you and the families in your program to reflect on. Field trips give you an opportunity to build your relationships with families and give the children in your care real life experiences that are priceless.

16

Continuing Professional Development

No matter what background and education you bring to your work with children, you should maintain a commitment to professionalism and continue learning about the care of young children. The child care profession has evolved over the years, and it continues to offer many types of educational and training opportunities for caregivers and assistants. Many states are mandating more training for child care staff. It is imperative that you seek out professional development opportunities in order to be a true professional in the early childhood field. Take advantage of the many available resources, such as local workshops, Internet training sessions, and child care conferences.

Be a Professional

A true early childhood professional has the ability to speak the language of and educate parents and the community about the early childhood profession. Careers in early childhood are often thought of as mediocre work, and most professionals in this field are not well compensated for the wonderful work they do to serve children and families. It is our professional responsibility to show the world, through our work and actions, the quality care we provide. We can support young children by joining with child advocacy organizations and speaking up on behalf of early childhood education. Our work with young children sets the foundations for their lifetimes of learning.

The families we serve and the community at large will appreciate our work more when we educate them on the importance of quality child care services. Quality child care includes the professionalism that both you and your assistants bring to your program. It involves a commitment to be your best and present yourself in a manner that is respected and responsible. The first impression of you and your child care business goes a long way in showing your professionalism. There are many ways to present a professional appearance. Here are several tips to help make your professionalism shine:

- Your passion for children should be proudly displayed within your environment. You can showcase the love you have for children by just being yourself. You can also wear special pins or T-shirts advocating for children. Place photos in your environment that portray you and the children joined together on a project or at an event.

- Wear attire that is respectful of the parents and children. It is difficult to play with the children in a mini skirt or slippers. Dress for success in child care. Wear comfortable, neat clothing that conveys your respect for the career you have chosen.

- Written and verbal communication should speak volumes about how well you can articulate pertinent information to your families. Effective communication is key to a lasting professional relationship with your families. Ensure that any memos, newsletters, or bulletin boards have been proofread and checked for accuracy and clarity.

- A quick response to an issue or conflict plays a huge part in accountability and demonstrates a commitment to your profession. Don't dodge problems or uncomfortable situations. Deal with them as they arise to maintain your credibility.

- A great professional attitude and a warm smile work wonders with everyone.

- Limit personal phone calls until after closing.

- Have limited contact with other adults when children are in your care. You may have friends or family who don't take your work seriously, so they stop by unannounced to sit and chat. This is time you are spending away from the children, and it is an intrusion on their time with you. Plus it puts you at risk for a child accusing your guests of inappropriate conduct.

- Inform your child care families of any relatives or friends temporarily living with you, especially if for an extended period of time. You may also need to inform your state licensing agency.

- Please put away magazines or reading materials that are not related to child care.

- Do not watch movies or television shows for adults while the children are in care. Soap operas and reality shows can be recorded and then viewed after hours.

- Please ensure that all assistants have their cell phones and small electronic gadgets turned off during child care hours. There's nothing worse than a parent or child competing for attention with your assistant because they are listening to their headset.

- Reduce gossip and rumors by the parents and the staff to ensure a positive and supportive environment.

- Maintain confidentiality.

- Stay organized.

- Inform parents of upcoming workshops that may benefit their family.

- Post a calendar of events so parents can plan to participate.

- Share with your parents any knowledge you gained from a recent conference.

- Put away any personal items and set aside chores that are not part of the child care setting. This means, for example, not folding your family's laundry while your child care is open.

- While you are open for business, if possible, limit the children in the neighborhood from interacting with the children in your care. You don't want the potential liability of an injured neighborhood child or of a parent accusing the visiting child of inappropriate conduct.

- Give adequate notice when you are going to be closed for business. Parents depend on you each day. Be sure to help them find alternative care during your vacations or emergency closings.

- Open for business on time and be prepared to receive the children.

Join Professional Organizations: You Are Not Alone

We are fortunate to have national organizations that give support and direction to early childhood professionals, and these organizations speak to the public on behalf of early childhood professionals. There are several large organizations that use their membership to do advocacy work, unite early childhood professionals, and raise awareness of this industry.

- Association for Childhood Education International (ACEI)

- National Association for the Education of Young Children (NAEYC)

- National Association for Family Child Care (NAFCC)

- National Black Child Development Institute (NBCDI)

- Children's Defense Fund (CDF)

It is to your advantage to join the local affiliate of at least one of these organizations to receive the greatest benefits and networking opportunities. You will have an opportunity to make real change in your community and serve on committees. Becoming an advocate for children is rewarding. In addition to the organizations listed above, there may be state and local organizations in your community that can benefit you.

If you don't have a local child care organization in your area, start one yourself. Your child care organization can be created to meet the needs of your community. I, along with two other child care providers, started a child care organization: the Child Care Providers' Network. We created this organization because we believed that family child care providers can be isolated and need a network to discuss child care issues. Our group met once a month at a community center or a provider's home. Child Care Providers' Network encouraged continuing education and peer mentoring. We discussed grant assistance as well as rules and current legislation pertaining to child care. We developed workshops to help increase the quality of child care in our community. We were typical family child care providers who wanted to increase the quality of care and offer a support mechanism for family child care providers.

Pursue Educational and Career Paths

There are many types of early childhood education paths to pursue. Some of the more common programs are the Child Development Associate (CDA) and associate's and bachelor's degrees in early childhood education or early childhood development. Completing a program takes commitment, perseverance, and sacrifice. *Just remember that true success takes hard work!*

The early childhood field has become more diverse in its career offerings. While family child care is a very successful field, you may find that you want to pursue a different career in early childhood in the future. Here is a brief list of careers in the field:

- center director

- research analyst

- consultant

- area manager

- teacher

- early childhood book sales person

- early childhood marketing professional

- child care supply specialist

- vendor for early childhood materials

- child care advocate

- trainer

- speaker

- fundraising consultant

- coordinator for the Food Program

- grant writer

Going back to school often presents fears and anxiety. The best advice that I can give is to surround yourself with people who support your endeavors and will lend a hand to help you succeed.

Tips on Succeeding in School

- Meet with advisors from several colleges to determine which school is right for you. Ask about class schedules, course loads, prerequisites, admission requirements, financial assistance programs, and scholarships.

- Set up a timetable for completing all coursework.

- Don't overwhelm yourself with too many courses.

- Keep in contact with your advisors to determine if you are on the right path to reach your goals.

- Network with classmates by creating study sessions.

- Stay focused.

- Don't procrastinate on your assignments. Study whenever possible and stay on top of your work.

- Don't be afraid to ask for help. Most colleges have tutoring programs to assist you.

Some of you may feel that you have been out of school too long to pursue a degree in early childhood education. Squash that myth! Start out gradually by taking one course or workshop, and when you feel comfortable add additional courses to your schedule.

Some of you may also feel that you are just too busy to attend a class or work on a degree. You can do it! Take an assessment of everything that you do in a week. Prioritize your list of things to do. Taking a course or training workshop adds value to you as a person and as a professional. You will own the knowledge and expertise. The degrees and certificates will have your name imprinted on them. These accomplishments are priceless. Ask yourself "What can I change or remove from my weekly schedule to include a two- to three-hour course?" Make you a priority. Remember, you are going to receive the initial benefit from attending school. The children in your care will benefit the most from the knowledge you gain and the creative activities and lessons you have experienced from others in the field.